VELASQUEZ

SPRING ART BOOKS

Velasquez

BY PHILIP TROUTMAN

SPRING BOOKS · LONDON

ACKNOWLEDGMENTS

The paintings in this volume are reproduced by kind permission of the following collections and galleries to which they belong: Frick Collection, New York (Plate 31); Galleria Doria Pamphili, Rome (Plate 37); Hispanic Society of America (Plate 11); Kunsthistorisches Museum, Vienna (Plates 39, 40, 41, 42, 46, 47); The Rt Hon The Earl of Radnor (Plate 36); Metropolitan Museum of Art, New York, Bequest of Benjamin Altman, 1913 (Plate 12); Musée des Beaux-Arts, Orleans (Plate 8); Museo del Prado, Madrid (Plates 6, 9, 13, 14, 15, 16, 17, 20, 21, 22, 23, 24, 25, 26, 28, 29, 30, 32, 33, 34, 38, 43, 44, 45, 48); Museum of Fine Arts, Boston (Plates 10, 18); the Trustees of the National Gallery, London (Plates 1, 3, 19, 35); National Galleries of Scotland (Plate 4); Wallace Collection, London (Plate 27); Wellington Museum, London (Plates 5, 7); Mrs Phyllis L. Woodall and Miss Frere (Plate 2). The black and white photographs in this volume are reproduced by kind permission of: the Trustees of the British Museum, London (Figure 5); Musée Condé, Chantilly (Figure 2); Museo del Prado, Madrid (Figures 1, 7); Museo Provincial de Bellas Artes, Granada (Figure 3); Museo Provincial de Bellas Artes, Valencia (Frontispiece); the Trustees of the National Gallery, London (Figure 6); Seville Cathedral (Figure 4). The following photographs were supplied by Ampliaciones y Reproducciones Mas, Madrid: Plate 25, Frontispiece, Figures 3, 4; Anderson-Giraudon, Paris: Figures 1, 7; Photographie Giraudon, Paris: Figures 2; Editions d'Art Albert Skira: Plate 37; Michael Holford, London: Plates 1, 2, 3, 5, 6, 7, 9, 13, 14, 15, 16, 17, 19, 20, 21, 22, 23, 24, 26, 27, 28, 29, 30, 32, 33, 34, 36, 38, 43, 44, 45, 48; Joseph P. Ziolo—André Held, Paris: Plates 39, 46.

Published by
SPRING BOOKS
Drury House • Russell Street • London
© Paul Hamlyn Ltd 1965
Printed in Czechoslovakia by Svoboda, Prague
T 1577

CONTENTS

BLACK AND WHITE ILLUSTRATIONS

INTRODUCTION

It is difficult to avoid a certain sense of the inevitable or predestined in the life and work of Velasquez.

His life has little drama to offer. There was never any material need for struggle, and he suffered no great personal misfortunes. He was blessed with a harmonious domestic life, with children (we meet his young wife and their first child in one of his earliest paintings, the *Adoration of the Kings*, Plate 6), and with grandchildren (his daughter with her children, and with Velasquez working on his last canvas, appear in the family portrait in Vienna painted by his pupil and son-in-law Mazo).

The progress of his painting is constant and unhurried, and almost imperceptible, and we are reminded of his own serious and reflective temperament — Philip IV referred to his 'phlegmatic' disposition. The same reflective temperament is to be observed in his earliest works, such as the *Christ in the House of Martha and Mary* (Plate 1 and Figure 6), as in the *Las Meninas* (Plate 43), the masterpiece of his last years. But in the forty years that separate these two works he advanced perhaps farther than any other painter.

The successive triumphs of his official career seem to take the same quiet and inevitable course: the immediate acceptance of the young painter at the Court of Madrid, and his triumph a few years later over all the established painters at the Court; his recognition by Rubens, the great painter of European fame, before he had reached thirty years of age, and his subsequent recognition 'by all the artists in Rome'; and at the very end of his career, his investiture as a Knight of the Order of Santiago.

A knowledge of his early years in Seville is all-important to an understanding of his painting. When young he was taught to look to nature for everything, and his trust in her lasted to the end.

Diego Rodríguez de Silva y Velázquez was born in Seville in 1599. His parents were well-to-do citizens of the town, and his father could claim noble descent through the de Silvas. The painter assumed his mother's name (Velázquez, in the proper Spanish form), a practice not uncommon in Andalusia.

Seville, as the port of the Spanish Americas, had grown over the past century to become the wealthiest and most cosmopolitan town of Spain, and the leading religious and cultural centre; and in the first decades of the seventeenth century it was to be the training ground of the great painters of Spain's Golden Age, the *Siglo de Oro*, for it was in Seville that Zurbarán and Cano of Velasquez' generation were trained, and two decades later, Murillo and Valdés Leal. The period more or less coinciding with Velasquez' career was the final phase of the *Siglo de Oro*, which produced such splendid achievements in the arts (Cervantes died in 1616; the poets and playwrights Góngora and Quevedo, both portrayed by Velasquez, and Lope de Vega and Calderón, were at the Court of Madrid when Velasquez was working there), also witnessed Spain's steady material decline, and finally the complete collapse both materially and spiritually of the most powerful nation in the world. In the early years of the seventeenth century, however, there could have been no premonition of the sorrowful events for Spain that were to follow, and the atmosphere of Seville must have been stimulating.

Velasquez apparently very early showed an aptitude for drawing, and when he was only eleven years of age, his parents decided to place him as apprentice for six years to the most highly esteemed master of Seville, Francisco Pacheco. The young apprentice was to stay in the house of Pacheco, who was responsible not only for his training as a painter, but also for his general education and upbringing. From the early eighteenth century, when Palomino, the then leading painter at the Court of Madrid, made reference, in his *El Museo Pictórico* (1724), to Pacheco's studio as a 'golden cage of art', the master has been much maligned, and it has been common to deny the salutary effect of his training. Apparently, too, in Pacheco's time there were those who begrudged his claim to have been the master of so remarkable a pupil. The fact is, Velasquez' parents made a happy choice, if prompted more by a consideration of prestige than by discernment. Palomino tells us that Velasquez' first master for a few months was Francisco Herrera the Elder. Herrera, who was born in the 1580s and had possibly himself been a pupil of Pacheco, was by all accounts a man proud and violent in disposition and one who was not ready to recognise or encourage the talent of others, and he appears completely opposed in temperament both to Pacheco and to his quiet and serious charge. If Palomino is right, the solid beginnings of Velasquez' painting indicate that he learned little from this initial short apprenticeship at the age of ten or eleven years, or soon realised the incompatibility of Herrera's interests and his own.

The devout Pacheco, a mediocre and conventional painter, but a man of great erudition, a poet, and one of the leading figures in Seville's cultural life, whose house was the meeting place of men of religion, scholars and artists, was ready to recognise genius in others and delighted in the company of men of worth 'who honoured the Spanish nation'. He appears to have been an excellent teacher, sympathetic of new ideas; he rejoiced in the discovery of his young pupil's genius, and admired and encouraged his quiet and serious industry; and, as his detailed treatise on painting, the *Arte de la Pintura* (published 1649), tells us, was able to give to Velasquez a thorough training in the craft of painting.

8

The style of painting in vogue in Spain in the later sixteenth century, inspired more by the authority of Italian theory than by a first-hand acquaintance with the art of Italy, and of which Pacheco (born in 1564) was a representative, had never really taken root in Spain. At the turn of the sixteenth century this imported style was giving way to a style based on naturalism and more Spanish in inspiration, exemplified by the still-lifes of Sánchez Cotán (Figure 3), painted around 1600. Even Pacheco was not unaffected by the new atmosphere and in his learned treatise — which includes a contemporary account of Velasquez' career to about 1632 — he insists on the prime necessity of a study of nature, and this formed the essential basis of Velasquez' art as it did of Baroque art, that is to say, of the specific style of the seventeenth century. 'I would go to nature for everything,' says Pacheco. 'Thus did Caravaggio, as can be seen by the copies of the *Crucifixion of Saint Peter*, and thus does Ribera [the great Spanish painter from Valencia, born in 1591, who worked in Spanish Naples and was in his early years a follower of Caravaggio], for his figures and heads appear alive . . . ; and my son-in-law [Velasquez] follows this path.'

Accounts of Caravaggio's new art, which at the beginning of the seventeenth century had introduced into Italy a style of naturalism that was the starting point for the development of Baroque painting, must have reached Spain and Seville by the second decade of the century, for it is precisely at that time — the time that Velasquez was to receive his first impressions — that we detect a sudden impetus in Spain's previously independent development on similar lines. Many times in his book Pacheco is enthusiastic about the new qualities of Caravaggio's paintings. The imposition of a violent contrast of light and shade stressed the plastic or three-dimensional quality of things, and this quality of relief is considered by Pacheco to be 'the most important part of painting'; and he cites again, among the artists whose paintings display this quality, Caravaggio and the Spanish Ribera. Whilst it is known that no paintings by Caravaggio himself had reached Seville, works by imitators or followers must have reached the town, for a mere acquaintance with a verbal account of the Italian's new painting would not seem to explain certain early works by Velasquez. Caravaggio's significant contribution was to confirm and encourage Spanish painting in the course it had already taken.

Except at the Court of Madrid, where there was also an important tradition of portrait painting going back to the mid-sixteenth century, there was in Spain little tradition other than for religious art, and even that was restricted to what may broadly be called the painting of images — of the central Mysteries and personages of the Faith. Pacheco was primarily a religious painter, but a central interest, too, in his life was portraiture — he was compiling his *Libro de Retratos*, a vast collection of drawings of the eminent men of his time — and he may well have imparted some of this interest to his pupil, who was to become the great portrait painter of all time.

In 1617, a few months after his apprenticeship ended, Velasquez matriculated as a *pintor de imaginería*, that is, a 'painter of religious images', the most important class of painter. Such a painter was not only responsible for painting religious images on panel or canvas, but also for the painting, or polychromy, of the carved wooden images in relief or in the round provided by the sculptor. There was a special intimate relationship between sculptor and painter in the production of the polychromed wooden images made for the retables of the chapels and for use in processions. Pacheco tells us that 'painting is the life of sculpture', and upon it 'depends the ultimate perfection of sculpture, that true imitation of nature'.

The effect of this relationship was to give to the painter not so much a feeling for form as a special feeling for his own material and an interest in naturalism. For the development of Spanish polychromed sculpture was the outcome of popular religious feeling, which demanded reality in the representation of the central persons of the Faith and their acts. Around 1600, so Pacheco tells us, the method of painting sculpture was revised. Such unrealistic treatment as, for example, the use of gold for the hair, was proscribed, for the intention of the polychromy was to achieve an effect of reality. The same materials were to be used as for painting on panel or canvas. There was in Spain at this time a general concern to achieve an impression of reality, and the new ideas were certainly debated in Pacheco's house.

A document from the year 1603 eloquently expresses the fundamental concern of the Baroque to involve the spectator:

Christ is to be shown alive, at the moment before He expires, with His head fallen on His right shoulder, and looking towards whomsoever should be praying at His feet, so that it will appear that Christ Himself addresses him, saying that it is for him that He suffers thus . . .

— so runs a clause in the contract for the *Crucified Christ* in Seville Cathedral carved by Montañés (1568—1649), a contemporary of Pacheco and the greatest sculptor of Spain at the time (Figure 4). This was by no means an isolated expression in early seventeenth-century Spain of the later endeavours of Baroque art to involve the spectator. To satisfy this demand for a heightened reality that was almost explicit in the contract, an artist required the full development of Baroque art, and Montañés' first great work does not achieve this. Velasquez, who was to achieve that Baroque quality of presence as no other artist, recalls magnificently the spirit of the contract in his *Crucified Christ* (Plate 25), painted in the 1630s.

In 1618, the year after Velasquez' matriculation as a master, Pacheco gave him his daughter, Juana, in marriage, 'guided by his industry and the great promise of his genius'; and five years later Velasquez left Seville for good for the Court of Madrid.

His father-in-law's account of his early activity in Seville and his paintings of this time give us a picture of a young man of exceptional talent, reflective and industrious. His works in Seville are characterised by a marked naturalism and a strong plasticity, and already give intimations of his 'painterly' instincts and his interest in the portrait. The term 'painterly' refers to that part of painting that is the concern more especially of the painter, that is to say, colour, tone, the handling of paint, as distinct from line or form, which are the concern more especially of the draughtsman or sculptor.

10

The youthfully fresh *Virgin of the Immaculate Conception* and *Saint John Evangelist on Patmos* (Plates 2 and 3), possibly the earliest paintings known by his hand and probably painted in 1617 as his first commission as a master, reveal a careful study of the model and a painter's delight in the actual substance and manipulation of the heavily applied paint, probably deriving from his training as a *pintor de imagineria*.

His *bodegones* (scenes of the kitchen or the market stall, with still-life; the term is nowadays equivalent to still-life) tell us even more about his interests at this time. 'It was through these beginnings, the painting of *bodegones*, a class of painting that certainly merits the highest praise if they are painted as my son-in-law paints them, and through his portraits, that he attained that true imitation of nature,' as Pacheco tells us. Some seven or eight *bodegones* have come down to us, all painted between about 1617 and 1620, including the early *Christ in the House of Martha and Mary*, the slightly later *The Cook* of 1618, the *Two men at a table* and the *Waterseller* (Figure 2, and Plates 1, 4, 5 and 7). The still-life objects and the models that recur in these paintings were always at hand; and the *bodegones*, not made for commission, provided an invaluable exercise for the young painter. In them he employs a restricted palette — earth browns, buffs and greys, and white — which he was unable to do in the few religious paintings that were commissioned to him, for the traditional colours to be used in the devotional image were laid down. This restricted palette enabled him to concentrate on the development of a composition by tonal relationships, which was to be fundamental to his method of painting. It was specifically a painter's approach, this relating things together in space by tone, and essential to his endeavours to create the impression of a reality of space and atmosphere. It is indeed only very gradually that he extends the range of his colours.

The still-life detail in the early *Christ in the House of Martha and Mary* (Plate 1), as in all these early paintings, already shows a painter's interest in the diverse qualities of things. This still-life is incredible for its time as the work of so young an artist, and there seems to be in his approach something of the objective attitude of the mature Dürer on his Netherlands journey. There is a similar objective approach to the portrait in these early works. The two figures from the *Christ in the House of Martha and Mary* suggest that he may even have known some page from Dürer's sketchbook of his Netherlands journey (Figure 2); Pacheco, at least, knew and admired Dürer's portrait drawings and engravings and set them as examples to follow. The boy in *The Cook* (Plate 4), who appears in other paintings at the time, may well be that 'country lad' that Pacheco tells us his son-in-law hired to serve as a model 'in different attitudes, smiling and weeping, without experiencing any difficulty'; whilst Velasquez' young wife is possibly to be seen in the *Virgin of the Immaculate Conception* (Plate 2), and again with their newly-born child in the *Adoration of the Kings* (Plate 6).

The last-mentioned work, painted in 1619, is the one which, in its stronger use of chiaroscuro, most readily brings Caravaggio to mind; but here, as in all his early paintings, there is a subduing of the Caravaggesque qualities, and there is nothing of the comparative violence of Caravaggio's paintings in his introduction of common types, in his employment of light, or in his modelling of the forms.

Before he left Seville he had painted at least two independent portraits, both dated in 1620, one of which is the *Jerónima de la Fuente* (Plate 9) which foreshadows something of the directness and simplicity of his later portraits painted at the Court of Madrid.

In Seville he had clearly stated his predilection for the portrait and expressed his essentially painterly instincts; he had built upon an intimate study of nature a solid foundation for his art which was to remain with him; and had initiated the steady tempo of his progress, which his acquaintance with the paintings in the royal collections at the Spanish Court and his visits to Italy could not disturb. But he had an immense distance to go.

In 1622, he made a preliminary visit to the Court of Madrid, 'desiring to see the Escorial', and sought an opportunity to paint the young Philip IV who had ascended the throne the year before. It was on this occasion that he painted for Pacheco the portrait of the poet *Góngora* (Plate 10). This first portrait painted at the Court already shows a significant advance: the comparatively literal description of features of his Sevillian portraits (Plate 9) begins to disappear in this portrait with its broader and more simplified treatment in planes. This was something new. The effect is both more natural and more impressive, and it was probably inspired by a consideration of his new subject, for his Sevillian works had still something of a youthful air which was inappropriate to the portrayal of the great poet and Chaplain of the King. This new treatment derives from his way of observing things by reference to light, and each subsequent extension of his technique depends on some new observation similarly made. In this instance, he observes the varying quality of light on an object according to the different angles subtended to the light of the different planes. Velasquez does not first draw the outlines of the objects he knows to be there and then model the forms by the imposition of a light and shade that he has not observed, but he observes the forms and records them through the medium of light, allowing the light to reveal the forms. He does not see objects divorced from the light or from the air or atmosphere in which they exist. This approach gives a reality to the light, and a heightened reality to the objects.

This initial journey to the Court was not without results, for in the following year he was called there by Juan de Fonseca, a high official of the Court, on the order of the Count-Duke of Olivares, the King's Favourite and Chief Minister. Velasquez' success was immediate. The portrait he made of his host Juan de Fonseca was taken to the Palace to be seen by the King and his Court, and at the first opportunity he was ordered to paint the King (Plate 12). A month later, in October, he was appointed the King's Painter, and so satisfied was the King with his first portrait that it was decided that Velasquez alone would be permitted in future to paint his likeness. Henceforth, Velasquez was to devote himself chiefly to portrait painting.

In 1627, he was appointed Usher to the Chamber, the first of a series of posts extraneous to his art with which he was to be honoured, and which brought him into more intimate contact with the King and life at the Court. Given his temperament, there can be no doubt that his favoured position, the atmosphere of the Court with its quiet and elaborate etiquette, and especially the respect for his painting and regard for his person shown by the King, who made no demands on his art, offered ideal conditions for the development of his genius.

The royal collections, rich in Venetian paintings, and especially the tradition of portrait painting at the Spanish Court, derived in part from Titian, must have been an inspiration to the artist who was to attain such mastery as a portrait painter and to become a painter as *painter* without peer; but one can point to no specific influence, nor indeed can one detect any sudden acceleration in the progress of his painting. The Venetian colour and technique was quite distinct from anything that Velasquez attained. Velasquez only introduced a comparable range of colour late in his painting and his palette never contained the rich and warm colouring of Venice; and his technique was not a manner that could be learned from art, but naturally derived from his observations before nature. It is true that the general idea for the pose of his portrait of the King was borrowed from the tradition at Court, but the simplicity of the pose and setting and the sobriety of colour were his own.

For some time black had been prescribed for the dress at the Spanish Court, and now on the accession of Philip IV and on the arrival of Velasquez at the Court, sumptuary regulations further simplified the dress worn at the Court, the elaborate ruffs worn in the previous reign being replaced by the simple *golilla* (collar). The sombre elegance of the dress was an expression of the atmosphere at the Court of Madrid, and it was of real significance to the artist who was to be the Court portrait painter. In these first years at the Court his palette was to remain restricted — buffs, browns, greys and white predominate, and now the black of the Court costume — but it becomes less heavy as he develops his composition in tone and gradually substitutes a natural and overall light for the more artificial lighting and chiaroscuro contrast of his Sevillian works; and the modelling of the forms becomes less hard as he continues to model increasingly by reference to light.

His paintings at this period include the various portraits of the King: the lost first portrait of 1623, the replica of 1624 (Plate 12), the lost equestrian portrait of 1625, and the portrait of the King standing of about 1626 (Plate 13); and the portraits of the King's Minister Olivares — one possibly painted in 1623, one painted in 1624 (now at São Paolo) and one in 1625 (Plate 11). The two latest portraits of the King and his Minister (Plates 11 and 13), with the enormous simplicity and impressive quality of their silhouettes, are the masterpieces of these early years at Court before he undertook his first visit to Italy.

A comparison between the *Góngora* of 1622 and the detail of the *Olivares* painted three years later (Plates 10, 11), and between the first portrait of the King and that of about 1626 (Plates 12, 13), will illustrate the progress made in these few years, in the more real treatment of light, the quieter modelling and the suggestion of atmosphere.

It has long been noticed that when Velasquez painted his later portrait of the King (Plate 13), he started with the lines of his lost first portrait recorded in the replica of 1624 (Plate 12). Oil paint becomes more transparent with time, and often, as in this case, reveals the *pentimenti* or changes made by an artist in the course of executing a painting. Recent X-ray photographs clearly show the pose of the early portrait, and have also suggested the possibility that the later portrait was painted over the actual 'lost' portrait. From now on, *pentimenti* appear in all his paintings, and it was in effect to be part of Velasquez' method of painting. That is to say, he was not to start by delineating the final contours of his design, later filling them in with paint — a method, nevertheless, that Pacheco seems to have favoured — but he allowed his final design to emerge gradually by constant adjustments in the course of painting. This again was specifically a painter's approach. It has led many to believe that Velasquez, who was constantly seeking perfection in his paintings, returned to them, sometimes years later, and made alterations.

It was in these years that Velasquez painted his first portrait of one of the Court Fools, that of '*Calabacillas*' (in the Cook Collection, Edinburgh), who some twenty years later was to be the subject of one of his most moving portraits (Plate 29). And around 1628 he painted for the King his first mythological painting, *The Drinkers* (Plate 14), representing Bacchus with his companions, in which he treats the classical subject-matter in terms of *genre*, as in Seville he had treated religious narrative as *genre* (see Figure 6). The more ambitious composition of *The Drinkers* lacks the unity of his single portraits painted at this time, and what strikes us most in the painting is the sympathetically observed group of drinkers on the right which has given the popular title to the painting. There is nothing of the traditional Italian heroic or lyrical interpretation of the mythological theme, such as Velasquez would have known from his acquaintance with the paintings in the royal collections, especially those of Titian and the Venetian masters. Henceforth, on the few occasions that he treated a mythological subject, it is to be in terms of everyday and present reality.

As long ago as 1492, the last of the Moors had been driven from Spain. Over a century later, in 1610, Philip III carried out his decision to expel the hundreds of thousands of converted Moors — 'Moriscos' — who had stayed on in the peninsula. The act was celebrated at the time in verse, and the King was hailed as a saint; but it proved to be one — and perhaps the most disastrous — of a series of misconceived policies in the reigns of Philip III and Philip IV that contributed to the economic decline of Spain. In 1627, it was decided to hold a competition among the painters of the Court, possibly following certain rumours of discontent at Velasquez' favoured position, and the subject chosen was the *Expulsion of the Moriscos*. The outcome was Velasquez' triumph over all the older and established painters at the Court. Palomino describes Velasquez' painting, now lost, which included an allegorical figure of Spain — a woman in Roman armour — presiding over the event. Velasquez must soon have realised that the incongruous allegorical figure, traditional in history painting, conflicted with his new approach which related everything to reality, and he never again introduced one.

From the autumn of 1628 to the spring of 1629, Rubens was at the Court of Madrid, sent on a diplomatic mission to help negotiate peace with England. The Flemish master is reported to have remarked on this occasion that he considered Velasquez the 'greatest living painter'. Velasquez, for his part, must have been inspired by Rubens' paintings (whose qualities were the reverse of that 'modesty' admired by Rubens in Velasquez' work), and must have wondered at the energy of Rubens, who in a short while at Court painted, among other things, the portraits of all the members of the royal household and 'made copies of all the Titians in the royal collections'. No other influence, however, can be detected from the meeting of these two men of such different temperaments — the young rising genius and the master of European fame. There appears, nevertheless, to have been one outcome, for it seems that Rubens encouraged Velasquez' desire to visit Italy, where at the same age as Velasquez he had studied with so much profit.

Later in the same year that Rubens left Madrid Velasquez undertook his first visit to Italy, for the purpose of study, returning to Spain at the beginning of 1631. He travelled in the company of the great Spanish general Ambrosio Spínola, Marquis de los Balbases, the victor of Breda, whom Velasquez was to portray later in his *Surrender of Breda* (Plate 21). Spínola, having been arbitrarily relieved of his highly successful command in the Netherlands, was reluctantly taking up his new post as military governor of the Spanish-ruled Milanese — yet another mistaken move by which Spain hoped to resolve her dilemma.

En route to Rome, where he spent most of his visit studying the works by the great Renaissance masters and others, he stayed a short while in Venice, where on account of the wars he was given an escort whenever he left his lodgings at the Ambassador's Palace to study the works of art in the city. Before returning to Spain he visited Naples, where he met the Spanish painter Ribera (born 1591), and on the order of the King painted the portrait of the King's sister, María, who was on her way to Hungary to marry the Emperor Ferdinand (the portrait is in the Prado).

It was apparently on this visit to Italy, when in the summer months he was staying at the Villa Medici in Rome, that Velasquez painted the two views of the *Medici Gardens* (Plates 16 and 17), in which he concerns himself with problems of space, light and atmosphere. These two small poetic landscapes, which so convincingly capture the specific quality of light of midday and evening, and are the only two independent landscapes certainly known by his hand, are to be counted among the most remarkable in the century which saw such progress in landscape painting. It was also in Rome that he painted the *Joseph's Coat* (in the Escorial), and his second mythological painting, *The Forge of Vulcan* (Plate 15), which illustrate the progress made in the portrayal of light and atmosphere, and hence space, in the few years after painting *The Drinkers* (Plate 14). A preoccupation at this time with problems of space, light and atmosphere was general to Baroque painting. Velasquez sought to represent space and depth by giving a reality of atmosphere. As he was unable to see objects divorced from light, so he was unable to see space divorced from light. To Velasquez, both objects and the space that surrounds them were things that more or less, and each in its own way, obstructed the light. He revealed objects, or figures, by painting the different qualities of the light that played on them, which will vary according to the form and surface qualities of the objects and the sources and degree of intensity of the light. The light may be intense or weak; it may be reflected, absorbed or scattered; and similarly, in its passage through the air, the light will vary in its qualities: its passage will be more or less impeded, it may combine or scatter in the air, be more or less active. By revealing both the objects and the space that surrounds them by reference to light, Velasquez gave a unity and a living quality to his representation of reality.

During Velasquez' absence from the Court of Madrid, a son and heir had been born to Philip IV, and the artist's first task on his return early in 1631 was to make the portrait of the young Prince, *Baltasar Carlos* (Plate 18); and soon afterwards, it seems, he was called upon to paint the so-called 'silver' portrait of the King, 'who had not been portrayed during his painter's absence' (Plate 19). Both portraits illustrate the advance made in the freedom of his technique and in the extension of his palette.

The first reports of the Count-Duke of Olivares' scheme to build another palace for Philip IV in Madrid date from the end of 1631. The Chief Minister wished to expedite the building of this edifice, the Buen Retiro Palace, conceived to entertain and enhance the prestige of the King. Already, in 1633, the *Gran Salón*, or Great Hall, was ready for its decoration. All the painters of the Court contributed to the decoration — even Zurbarán was brought from Seville to paint two battle-pieces and a series of the Labours of Hercules — which was completed two years later, in 1635. The grandiose scheme of decoration was planned to celebrate the military triumphs of Philip IV's reign — and was completed on the very eve of Spain's final military defeat. Velasquez' contribution included the five equestrian portraits of the reigning King, the Queen and the Prince, and Philip III and his Queen, and the *Surrender of Breda* (Plate 21), one of twelve battle-pieces.

The last-mentioned painting is the great central work of Velasquez' career, and is generally considered to be one of the masterpieces of history painting of all time. The event is sympathetically interpreted in purely human terms, and breaks completely with the tradition of history painting which treated such events as allegory or as a grand spectacle. The individuals involved in the event were of almost exclusive significance to Velasquez — the Dutch and Spanish troops, and more especially the respective commanders, Justin of Nassau and Ambrosio Spínola. Velasquez knew Spínola, whose action is the key to his interpretation of the event.

It is in this composition and in the equestrian portraits, in which the figures are posed in a spacious landscape against a distant view of the Guadarramas mountains, that Velasquez' style reaches its high-point in the expression of external movement and grandeur of effect. This coincides in time with a similar culmination in Baroque painting

16

1 VELASQUEZ.
The Adoration of the Kings.
Oil on canvas. 78⅞ × 49½ in.
(203 × 125 cm.). Dated 1619.
Museo del Prado, Madrid.

2 ALBRECHT DÜRER.
A page from the
Netherlands Sketchbook.
Drawing in silverpoint. 1520–1521.
Musée Condé, Chantilly.

3 JUAN SÁNCHEZ COTÁN.
Still-life.
Oil on canvas. *c.* 1600.
Museo Provincial, Granada.

generally. It has been denied that Velasquez was a Baroque artist, and it is true that there is none of the grand flourish, the exaggerated movement, the introduction of floating allegorical figures, that one sees in the works of the same time by the great master of the Baroque, Rubens. The reality of life of Velasquez' painting did not, however, require to be augmented by any rhetorical artifice.

Probably painted soon after the works for the *Gran Salón* of the Buen Retiro Palace is the *Crucified Christ*, his masterpiece in religious painting, which recalls Montañés' interpretation of the subject and the contract of 1603 already mentioned (Plate 25 and Figure 4).

The ultimate development of Velasquez' individual painting belongs to the succeeding two decades; and there follow upon the great series for the Buen Retiro Palace a number of highly personal works in which his interpretation of the portrait of the individual is finally solved. The first great masterpiece of this final phase is formed by the series of four portraits of Court Fools painted around 1644 (Plates 29, 30, 32 and 33) and the so-called 'Fraga' portrait of the King painted in that year at Fraga, when Velasquez accompanied Philip IV to the battle-front in Aragon (Plate 31). The King, painted in the red and silver uniform he wore on the campaign and holding the marshal's baton, could appropriately have been portrayed in the grand manner of the equestrian portraits painted for the decoration of the Buen Retiro Palace. But the portrait is both more sympathetic and stronger in its appeal for its exclusive concentration on the King, without the inclusion of any accessories. Velasquez was not to repeat the spacious settings of his great works of the mid-1630s, but was now to concentrate more exclusively on the sitter, and relate the space more intimately to the portrait.

The series of four Court Fools is probably, for all the humble character of the sitters, the most splendid single portrait series produced in the Baroque age. There is no attempt at caricature and no attempt to enlist our pity, but only an equal, profound and sympathetic portrayal of each of them as a person. No other painter has succeeded in giving so powerful and quiet a sense of presence and inner life to the simple portrayal of an individual. As with the portrait of the King, the single figure alone is presented to us; and each figure is shown in an ordinary and natural light and atmosphere, but one which is most appropriate to his character, or best brings out his character.

Other paintings to be dated between the late 1630s and 1648, when he again left Spain for Italy, include the *Mars* (Plate 34), which seems finally to state the Spanish lack of sympathy for the Italian humanist conception of the pagan deity; the *Venus* (Plate 35), which is certainly a portrait, and knows little of classical ideas of beauty and proportion; and the *Menippus* and *Aesop* (Plate 28). His interpretation of the two 'beggar-philosophers', Menippus and Aesop, is in completely contemporary and Spanish terms, that of the *pícaro* — the subject of the picaresque novel — a figure essentially not of burlesque or fantasy, but of reality and significance, a characteristic human and social phenomenon of this period of a great nation's decline: as always, Velasquez' interpretation is in real terms.

In 1648 he made another journey to Italy, again visiting Venice and Naples and staying most of the time in Rome. He returned to the Court in the middle of 1651. This time he was sent as Ambassador Extraordinary on a mission to acquire paintings and sculptures, to have casts made of the more important antique sculptures, and to arrange for frescoists to come to Spain, for alterations were being made in the Royal Palace and the new apartments needed decorating and furnishing. There was a prestige value in antique sculptures, and understandably very few of these not easily transportable objects had left Italy. Developments in the technique of casting now made it possible, if one could not acquire the originals, to form a collection of the more famous works. In Spain, too, there was no native tradition for the Italian technique of fresco painting. Spain's first real contact with the art of Italy was made in the sixteenth century, and at that time her demands for fresco painting were almost all satisfied by Italian painters. A more cogent reason at this time for bringing in Italian frescoists was the high reputation they had deservedly gained in the seventeenth century by their grand achievements in the field of illusionistic ceiling decoration. The most famed of all was Pietro da Cortona (1596—1669) whom Velasquez was ordered to invite to Spain, but the King was to be disappointed.

Velasquez' mission in Italy clearly took up a proportion of his time, but he had ample opportunity in the two and a half years to paint, and among the number of portraits he made in Rome (most of which are lost) are the *Innocent X* (Plate 37), with its brilliant technique and colour, and its deep penetration of character and powerful presence, and the portrait of Velasquez' assistant *Juan de Pareja* (Plate 36). Reynolds considered the *Innocent X* to be the greatest portrait in Rome, and it will remain one of the supreme masterpieces both of portraiture and painting.

In 1651 Velasquez returned to a changed Court. The King's first wife, Queen Isabel, had died in 1644, and the Prince Baltasar Carlos, the only heir to the Spanish Crown, in 1646. During Velasquez' absence in Italy, Philip IV had married his young niece, Mariana, his sister María's daughter, and a few days after Velasquez' arrival at Court, in the middle of 1651, the Infanta Margarita was born. During the eight years of activity left to him after his return to Madrid and before his death in 1660, the painter's main task was the portrayal of the young Queen, the young Princess, and later the short-lived Philip Prosper on whom the King's hopes for an heir were placed. These portraits constitute a series of masterpieces of colour and handling and sympathetic portraiture (Plates 38 to 42 and 46 and 47), and culminate in his final masterpiece, *Las Meninas*, 'The Maids of Honour' (Plate 43), a portrait of the royal family centred on the young Princess, the Infanta Margarita, painted in 1656, in which he captures the whole atmosphere of the Court, and, one feels, something of the atmosphere of Spain of the time. A sense of melancholy seems inseparable from the deep sympathy of his approach and from the very reality of the scene — that moment in the life of the Court so grandly captured — and from the very perfection of the technique.

It is generally considered that *The Spinners* (Plate 44 and Figure 7) was painted at this time. *The Spinners* is the popular title, and the painting actually tells the story of Pallas and Arachne, a fable of pride, in which Arachne dares to compete with the goddess Pallas, and for her presumption is changed into a spider. The story is told by reference to an ordinary scene in the Royal Tapestry Factory in Madrid; and, as in *Las Meninas*, there is that so real and yet so magical quality of light, which seems in this case actually to interpret the myth. This is the painting before which Mengs exclaimed: 'It seems as if the hand took no part in the execution.' Anton Raphael Mengs (1728—1779), the great European painter and theorist from Bohemia, who had worked in so many of the Courts in Europe, and finally, from 1761, at the Court of Madrid, was the propagator of the new classical ideas of the eighteenth century, whose theories were apparently so opposed to the radical naturalism of Velasquez' art. Yet it was Mengs who was the first to attempt a discerning appraisal rather than a eulogy of Velasquez' painting, and his remark voices the reaction of men of every persuasion who have made the acquaintance of Velasquez' paintings. For Velasquez' paintings can seem to be, as it were, a natural phenomenon, to be reality itself; not a reality of things alone, but of existence. And these final masterpieces by his hand contain something of the mystery and deep human significance of existence.

Velasquez' last portrait of the King, whose reign, one can say, coincided with that of his painter, is the final page of one of the most penetrating biographies of a man (Plate 48; and see Plates 12, 13, 19, 20 and 31).

The pair of portraits of the young *Infanta Margarita* and *Prince Philip Prosper* (Plates 46 and 47), painted in 1659, are two of the most sympathetic portraits of children ever painted, and were, as Palomino puts it, 'the last of his paintings, and the last in perfection'. They fitly close his career.

At the end of the year 1659 Velasquez was given the final honour of being made a Knight of the Order of Santiago; and in the spring of the following year he made the journey to the Isle of Pheasants, on the frontier of Spain and France, to help prepare as *Aposentador* of the King the celebrations for the meeting of the Spanish King with Louis XIV of France and the giving in marriage of the Spanish Princess María Teresa to the French King. After witnessing this act symbolic of Spain's final decline, Velasquez made the arduous return journey to Madrid, and shortly after his arrival at the Court fell ill. In the first days of August he died, mourned by his royal patron and friend.

It was inevitable that so individual an artist should have had no real following. During his lifetime a number of assistants, of whom the most gifted was his son-in-law Mazo, were employed to make the many replicas of Velasquez' paintings to be sent to the various Courts of Europe; and his example gave rise to a whole school of portrait painting in Madrid, whose representatives included painters of some merit, but who were unable to repeat more than the external formulae of Velasquez' portraits.

His acceptance was immediate in his lifetime in Madrid where his paintings were seen; and subsequently all who became acquainted with his paintings have recognised their unique quality; but it was to be a long time before more than a few people had made this acquaintance. The Italian painter Luca Giordano (1632—1705), nicknamed *fa presto*, on account of the rapid execution of his paintings, who at the end of the seventeenth century painted as many figures on the ceiling of the Grand Stairway of the Escorial in a few weeks as Velasquez painted in a lifetime, called *Las Meninas* the 'Theology of Painting', meaning that 'as Theology is the greatest of the Sciences, so Velasquez' painting is the greatest in Painting'. Mengs' remark made in the 1760s has already been quoted; and likewise Reynolds' admiration of the portrait of *Innocent X* which he saw in Rome. But these were isolated instances, and Velasquez remained effectively unknown outside Spain until the nineteenth century.

The Romantic movement turned its attention to Spain and to countries farther afield, and Delacroix early in the nineteenth century grappled with his copy of one of Velasquez' paintings. To Théophile Gautier and to the Realists in the middle of the century the reality of Velasquez' painting was a revelation. Later in the century the Impressionists looked especially to Velasquez' technique. R. A. M. Stevenson, a spokesman of the Impressionists, in his *Art of Velasquez* (1895), was perhaps the first to notice the identification of Velasquez' technique with the whole approach and meaning of his art:

> 'varying his manner of painting [that is, his technique] according to the sentiment of his impression, so that you will find no pattern of brush-work, no settled degree of intimacy in the modelling, . . . and in short, no fixed habits or methods of expression'.

Manet more especially among the Impressionists, studied the great Spanish master, and in his final masterpiece, the *Bar aux Folies-Bergère* (Courtauld Institute Galleries, London), painted in 1882 shortly before he died, he seems to make reference to Velasquez' final masterpiece, *Las Meninas*. In 1957, three hundred years after Velasquez painted *Las Meninas*, Picasso paid homage to his great countryman when he painted his series of forty-four variations on Velasquez' painting. In 1960, the Spanish playwright Antonio Abuero Vallejo contributed the play *Las Meninas* to the tercentenary celebrations in Spain of Velasquez' death. As a prelude to the play, Velasquez' two 'beggar philosophers' (see Plate 28) stand before us as in Velasquez' paintings, and as one, Menippus, quietly breathes the words: '*...Estamos vivos...*', ('Yes, we live . . .') they begin to live. And as we stand before Velasquez' paintings, the individuals of his world — the King, the dwarfs, the children, eternalised by his brush — seem to breathe, to live, to present to us their souls.

OUTLINE BIOGRAPHY OF VELASQUEZ

Francisco Pacheco (1564—1644) in his *Arte de la Pintura* (1649) gives a contemporary account of Velasquez' career to about 1632. Antonio Palomino (1653—1728), who was the leading painter at the Spanish Court in the early eighteenth century, includes in his *El Museo Pictórico* (1724) the first full biography of Velasquez. The references 'Pacheco' and 'Palomino' are to the *Arte de la Pintura* and *El Museo Pictórico* respectively.

6TH JUNE 1599   Diego Rodríguez de Silva y Velázquez, son of Juan Rodríguez de Silva and his wife Jerónima (née Velázquez), baptised in the parish church of San Pedro, Seville. His father's parents had moved to Seville from Oporto in Portugal, possibly at the time that Portugal became part of Spain in 1580.

1610—1611   According to Palomino, Velasquez spent a few months with the Sevillian painter Francisco Herrera the Elder before entering the studio of Pacheco. If true, it must have been in 1610 or 1611. Pacheco's apparent denial that his pupil had any other master appears rather to confirm Palomino's statement: '*And because it is a greater honour to have been the master than to have been the father-in-law, I feel justified in refuting the presumption of someone who would claim the glory of being his master, taking from me the crown of my last years.*'

17TH AND 27TH SEPTEMBER 1611   Contract of apprenticeship with Francisco Pacheco (born in Seville, 1564) for a period of '*six years dating from the 1st December of the preceding year*'. The reason for the backdating of the apprenticeship is not clear. Pacheco visited Madrid and the Escorial in 1611, and also visited Toledo to meet El Greco. Possibly, the signing of the contract was held over until Pacheco's return to Seville and it was during his master's absence that Velasquez spent the few months with Herrera.

1614   Zurbarán (born in Estremadura, 1598) starts his three years' apprenticeship as a painter in Seville with a Pedro Díaz de Villanueva.

17TH AUGUST 1616   The sculptor and painter Alonso Cano (born in Granada, 1602) enters Pacheco's studio as an apprentice.

28TH MAY 1617   Velasquez successfully examined as a *pintor de imaginería* by Pacheco and another

Sevillian painter; he is accepted as a master, and is now permitted to practise his art independently. His first commission as a master was possibly the *Immaculate Conception* and the *Saint John Evangelist* (Plates 2 and 3).

7TH MARCH 1618   Pacheco nominated Censor and Inspector of Sacred Paintings by the Inquisition.

23RD APRIL 1618   Marriage of Velasquez with Pacheco's daughter Juana (born end of May 1602): '*after five years of education and training, I gave him my daughter in marriage, moved by his virtue and good parts, and by the promise of his natural and great talent*' (Pacheco). Paints *The Cook* (Plate 4), his first certainly datable work.

MAY 1619   Birth of Velasquez' first daughter, Francisca.

In 1619 paints the *Adoration of the Kings* (Plate 6). His young wife and newly-born daughter are probably portrayed in the Virgin and the Christ Child.

1ST FEBRUARY 1620   Contracts of apprenticeship of Diego de Melgar, '*of thirteen to fourteen years of age*', with Velasquez, for a period of six years.

JUNE 1620   Paints the portrait of the nun *Jerónima de la Fuente* (Plate 9), and in the same year the posthumous portrait of *Suárez de Ribera* (Church of San Hermenegildo, Seville), possibly his first portrait commissions.

1621   On the 2nd March and the 13th June 1621 lets property in Seville, possibly in anticipation of his removal to Madrid.

14TH APRIL 1622   Gives powers to Pacheco to collect moneys on his behalf. In May, in Velasquez' absence, Pacheco lets property on his behalf.

SPRING 1622   Velasquez' first visit to Madrid and the Court: '*Desiring to visit the Escorial, he left Seville for Madrid in the month of April 1622. He made at my instance a portrait of Góngora* [Plate 10] *. . . There was no opportunity to paint the portrait of the King at the time, although he sought to . . .*' (Pacheco).

25TH JANUARY 1623   Again lets property in Seville.

SUMMER 1623   Second visit to the Court at Madrid, called by Philip IV's Chief Minister Olivares. His success is immediate, and he settles in Madrid as the King's painter. '*He was called to Madrid by Juan de Fonseca, by order of the Count-Duke, and stayed in his house and made his portrait* [lost, unless Olivares is intended] *. . . which was taken to the Palace that evening . . . and was seen by all, the Princes and the King. He was ordered to make a portrait of the Prince, but it appeared more appropriate to make the King's portrait first . . . and this was carried out on the 30th August to the satisfaction of the King, Princes and the Count-Duke* [this first portrait of the King is lost, but is recorded in the replica painted in 1624; see Plate 12] *. . . He also made a portrait of the Prince of Wales* [later Charles I of England, who was in Madrid seeking the hand of the King's sister, María; the portrait is lost], *for which he was given a hundred ducados . . . The Count-Duke . . . promised that he alone would be given permission to paint the King . . .*' (Pacheco).

6TH OCTOBER 1623   Nominated Royal Painter, at a salary of 20 ducados per month and with payment for paintings made in the service of the King. Later in the month his nomination and salary were confirmed after objections that there was no criterion for so high a remuneration.

4TH DECEMBER 1624	Velasquez paid on account for three portraits of *Philip IV* (Plate 12), *Olivares* (São Paolo) and *García Pérez* (lost), painted for Pérez' wife Antonia de Ipeñarrieta.
1625	Paints his (lost) first equestrian portrait of *Philip IV*: '*having finished the portrait of the King on horseback, in which he copied everything from nature including the landscape, it was the King's pleasure to exhibit the painting outside the church of San Felipe . . . of which I was witness*'. Pacheco was in Madrid to witness this triumph of his son-in-law, and he and other poets celebrated the event in verse. Pacheco refers to his young protégé as '*the Apelles of a greater Alexander*'. Palomino records that Velasquez eventually destroyed most of the painting, following criticism of the drawing of the horse, and that he changed the customary inscription '*pinxit*' ('painted') to '*expinxit*' ('painted out')! The bust portrait in the Prado, of the King in armour against a blue background, has been considered a fragment of the painting.
	Paints a portrait of *Olivares* (Plate 11).
7TH MARCH 1626	Velasquez solicits the post of Royal Painter for his father-in-law, on the death of one of the Royal Painters, but without any outcome.
1627	Paints his first history piece, *The Expulsion of the Moriscos* (lost), '*in competition with the three established painters at the Court, Vicente Carducho, Eugenio Caxés and Angelo Nardi, and is judged the best* [Carducho, the painter of most authority at the Court at the time, was born in Florence in 1576 and accompanied his brother to the Escorial in 1584; Caxés, the son of an Italian painter who had moved to Spain to paint in the Escorial, was born in Madrid in 1577; Nardi was born near Florence in 1584 and moved to Spain in 1607] . . . *and having succeeded against all in the opinion of those nominated by the King, Juan Bautista Crecencio and Juan Bautista Mayno* [architect and painter at the Court, respectively, both of Italian origin], *he was honoured with the office of Usher to the Chamber . . .; and to this was added the ration of 12 reales per day which is given to those attached to the Royal Chamber . . .*' (Pacheco). Documents confirm Pacheco's account. The post of Usher to the Chamber was the first of a series of posts extraneous to his art with which he was to be honoured.
3RD AUGUST 1627	Gives powers to Pacheco to sell property in Seville given him by his father-in-law as a dowry.
ABOUT 1628	On the 22nd July 1629, Velasquez was paid 400 ducados owing for paintings made in the service of the King, including the *Bacchus* (Plate 14). This, the first mythological painting, was probably painted the year before. About the same time he painted his first portrait of a Court Fool, the '*Calabacillas*' (Cook Collection, Edinburgh).
AUGUST 1628 — APRIL 1629	Rubens in Madrid on a diplomatic mission. '*Rubens was not much in the society of painters and only with my son-in-law, with whom he had corresponded previously, did he form a friendship, admiring his painting highly for its modesty, and together they visited the Escorial*' (Pacheco). Gaspar de Fuensalida, Keeper of the Rolls of the Golden Fleece at the Palace, in his testimony supporting Velasquez' eligibility for the Order of Santiago in 1659, made the statement that Rubens on this visit '*confessed that Velasquez was the greatest European painter*'.

28TH JUNE 1629 Given licence to travel to Italy. He was to receive in his absence *'the same salary and other payments as now'*.

AUGUST 1629— JANUARY 1631 Velasquez' first visit to Italy, undertaken for the purpose of study: *'In fulfilment of his great wish to visit Italy . . . the King, who had previously given his promise on a number of occasions, now gave him leave . . . giving him 400 ducados and two years salary . . . , the Grand-Duke giving him another 200 ducados and many letters of recommendation . . . He left Madrid with Spínola and embarked at Barcelona on the day of Saint Lawrence* [10th August] *1629. He stopped at Venice, where he stayed with the Spanish Ambassador . . . and because of the wars, guards were sent to accompany him whenever he left the Palace. Thence he passed through Ferrara . . . , and Cento . . . , to Rome, where he stayed a year . . . , the Cardinal Barberini arranging for him to have quarters in the Vatican Palace. He was given keys to some apartments . . . , and made drawings from the* Last Judgment *by Michelangelo and the paintings by Raphael . . . Later, considering the Villa Medici a suitable place in which to study and pass the summer . . . for there were many antique sculptures for him to copy, he asked the Spanish Ambassador to negotiate with Florence, and stayed there for more than two months, until a fever forced him to leave . . . Among the works he made in Rome is a remarkable Self-portrait which I have* [lost] *. . . Returning to Spain from Rome he visited Naples, and there painted the portrait of the Queen of Hungary* [the King's sister, María, who was in Naples from August to December 1630, on her way to Hungary to marry the Emperor Ferdinand III; the portrait is in the Prado] *to take to His Majesty. He returned to Madrid after a year and a half of absence, arriving at the beginning of 1631, and was well received by the Count-Duke who commanded him to present himself to the King, who had not had his portrait made during Velasquez' absence . . . , and was waiting for him to make a portrait of the Prince* [Baltasar Carlos, born 17th October 1629; Plate 18], *which he did immediately. It is incredible the generosity and friendship with which so great a monarch treated him; he had his studio in his Apartments, to which the King had a key, and a chair from which he could watch him paint, which he did almost every day. But what exceeded everything was that when he was painting the King on horseback, the King sat for three hours at a time* [apparently a reference to the lost portrait painted in 1625]' (Pacheco).

Pacheco's contemporary account of the Italian visit is supported by documents. Velasquez apparently especially mentioned the town of Cento to his father-in-law, where he would have met the painter Guercino (born 1591), for whose painting he seemed to have had some sympathy. In *The Spinners* (Figure 7; see Note to Plate 44) he made use of one of his studies of the Sistine Ceiling. Of the *Self-portrait*, now lost, Pacheco says on another occasion that it was *'in the manner of Titian; and if it is not improper to say so, Velasquez is not inferior to that master in his heads'*. Other paintings made in Rome at this time are the *Joseph's Coat* (the Escorial) and the *Forge of Vulcan* (Plate 15), and apparently the small painting recording a *Fight outside the Spanish Ambassador's Palace* (Palazzo Pallavicini, Rome). In Naples, Velasquez would have met for the first time the great Spanish painter Ribera (1591—1652).

26

5 FRANCISCO PACHECO.
Saint John Evangelist on Patmos.
Drawing in pen and wash.
Dated 1632.
British Museum, London.

4 JUAN MARTÍNEZ MONTAÑÉS.
The Crucified Christ
Polychromed sculpture in wood. Life-size.
1603—1606. Seville Cathedral.

6 VELASQUEZ.
Christ in the House of Martha and Mary.
Oil on canvas.
$23\frac{5}{8} \times 40\frac{3}{4}$ in. (60×103 cm.). *c.* 1617—1618.
National Gallery, London.

7 VELASQUEZ.
The Spinners (The Story of Pallas and Arachne). Oil on canvas.
85×114 in. (220×289 cm.). *c.* 1657?
Reproduced in its original form, without the later extension of the canvas at the top (see note on Plate 44). Museo del Prado, Madrid.

1631	Paints immediately on his return from Italy the *Baltasar Carlos and Dwarf* (Plate 18) as recorded by Pacheco; and possibly not long afterwards the National Gallery '*Silver*' *Philip* (Plate 19). The small *Crucified Christ* in the Prado is dated 1631. The larger *Crucified Christ* painted for the church of San Plácido, Madrid, his masterpiece iu religious painting, was probably painted a few years later.
24TH SEPTEMBER 1632	Conceded a *vara de alguacil* ('magistrate's rod': a constable of the Court, charged with collecting dues), a sinecure which would have brought him a small income from the person to whom he delegated the duties. In a document relating to this, Velasquez is referred to as '*Painter to the Chamber of the King and of the Count-Duke*'. He sells his *vara de alguacil* in 1634.
21ST AUGUST 1633	Velasquez' daughter, Francisca, is married to his assistant and pupil, Juan Bautista Martínez del Mazo.
30TH JANUARY 1634	Granted permission to transfer the office of Usher of the Chamber to Mazo '*who has married his daughter*'.
APRIL—NOVEM- BER 1634	Zurbarán in Madrid from Seville to paint for the Buen Retiro Palace.
1634—1635	Decoration of the *Gran Salón* of the Buen Retiro Palace, Madrid. On the 16th June 1635 Velasquez is paid 2500 ducados for his share of the work, which included the *Surrender of Breda*, the masterpiece of his middle period (Plate 21), and the equestrian portraits of *Philip IV*, *Prince Baltasar Carlos* (Plates 20 and 22), the reigning Queen Isabel, and Philip III and his Queen, the three last mentioned being adaptations by Velasquez of earlier paintings.
	Painted at the same time the equestrian portrait of *Olivares* (Prado).
JUNE 1635 — BEGINNING 1636	The Sevillian sculptor Montañés at the Court '*for over seven months*' from June 1635 to model a bust of the King to be sent to Pietro Tacca in Florence who was making an equestrian statue in bronze of the King, based on Velasquez' painting, for the Buen Retiro Palace.
	Velasquez painted Montañés working on the model of the King's head on this occasion (Plate 24).
OCTOBER 1635— OCTOBER 1636	*Prince Baltasar Carlos in hunting dress* (Plate 23) painted when the Prince was six years of age, according to the inscription on the painting. The two other 'hunting' portraits, also destined for the Torre de la Parada, the hunting lodge near Madrid, representing the *King* (the head is the same as that in the National Gallery '*Silver*' *Philip*) and the *Cardinal Infante Ferdinand*, were probably painted earlier, and before the works for the Buen Retiro Palace (the paintings are in the Prado). The *Boar Hunt* in the National Gallery, London, was also possibly painted at this time. The *Aesop* (Plate 28) and *Menippus*, and *Mars* (Plate 34), all in the Prado, were also painted for the Torre de la Parada, but are apparently later in date.
1636	Nominated Assistant to the Wardrobe.
	A recently discovered document seems to record Velasquez' presence in Rome in 1636; and in his testimony in support of the granting to Velasquez of the Order of Santiago

in 1658, Gaspar de Fuensalida, who held positions of honour at the Court, states that the King had sent Velasquez to Italy on three occasions. The visit could not have been of long duration, for his presence in Madrid is recorded a number of times in 1636.

24TH JANUARY 1638
Pacheco finishes his *Arte de la Pintura* (published posthumously in 1649).

AUTUMN 1638
Recorded as painting a lost portrait of the *Duchesse de Chevreuse*. Painted the portrait of Francesco d'Este I (Galleria Estense, Modena) when the sitter was in Madrid as god-father to the Infanta María Teresa (born in September, 1638).

12TH MARCH 1639
Fulvio Testi, the Modenese Ambassador in Madrid, writing to Francesco d'Este, says: '*I do not consider Velasquez' portraits inferior to those by any painter of greater renown past or present*'.

26TH MAY 1639
The Cardinal Infante Ferdinand writes from the Netherlands to his brother, Philip IV: '*I am madly content with the portrait of the Prince* [Baltasar Carlos]. *My portrait is finished, but the painters here in Flanders are more "phlegmatic" than Velasquez* [the opposite, apparently, of the King's appraisal of Velasquez' disposition].' The portrait of *Prince Baltasar Carlos* is not certainly known, and candidates for it include the more intimate version at Ickworth of the portrait of the Prince in hunting dress (see Plate 23) and the portraits of the Prince in Court dress and in armour recorded in paintings in Vienna and The Hague respectively.

In 1639 he signed and dated the portrait of *Admiral Adrián de Pulido Pareja*, known from the copy, probably by Mazo, in the National Gallery, London. Palomino relates how the King was taken in by the reality of the portrait. Entering Velasquez' studio one day, at the time that the Admiral was supposed to be absent from Madrid, he suddenly came across the portrait which was standing in an obscure part of the room, and upbraided the Admiral for not having left.

6TH JANUARY 1643
Nominated Assistant to the King's Chamber.

9TH JUNE 1643
Nominated Assistant Superintendent of Works for the King, at 60 ducados per month.

SUMMER 1644
Velasquez accompanies the King on his campaign to Aragon, when he paints the so-called '*Fraga' Philip* (Plate 31) at Fraga, where the King stopped on his way to the relief of Lérida, held by the French. On the same occasion he painted the '*El Primo*' (Plate 30), one of a series of four Court Fools (see Plates 29, 32 and 33), which constitute his greatest achievement before his second visit to Italy.

NOVEMBER 1644
Death of Pacheco in Seville.

22ND JANUARY 1647
Nominated Supervisor, and shortly afterwards also *Contador*, or Paymaster, of the new works on the building of the *Pieza Ochavada* (Octagon) in the Royal Palace.

ABOUT 1648
Painted the *Venus* (Plate 35) before leaving for Italy at the end of 1648, and probably not long before (Inventory of 1651).

NOVEMBER 1648
Velasquez visits Italy for the last time (his second visit, unless he had also been to Italy

JUNE 1651
in 1636): '*In 1648, Velasquez was sent by the King to Rome as Ambassador Extraordinary to Innocent X to buy works of painting and sculpture and to have casts made of the more*

famous Greek and Roman sculptures . . . He left Madrid in November 1648, and embarked at Málaga with the Duke of Nájara who was going to Trent to receive the new Queen Mariana [Queen Isabel had died in 1644, and Philip married his young niece, Mariana, in 1649; for her portrait see Plate 38]. *He disembarked at Genoa, and passed through Milan, where he did not stay to see the entry of the Queen . . . , and thence through Padua to Venice . . . , where he bought paintings . . . Thence to Bologna . . . , where he invited Mitelli and Colonna to Spain, . . . and thence to Florence . . . , Modena . . . , Parma . . . , and Rome, whence on his arrival he had to continue to Naples to see the Viceroy who was to give him the necessary assistance for his stay in Italy. Here he visited Ribera . . . , and returned to Rome . . . , where in addition to carrying out the mission of his visit he painted many things and especially the portrait of Innocent X* [his most celebrated single portrait; see Plate 37] *. . . , for which the Pope honoured him with a gold medallion . . . Before making the Pope's portrait he decided to practise his hand in painting a head, and made the portrait of Juan de Pareja* [Plate 36] *. . . , and as it was the custom on Saint Joseph's Day* [19th March] *to decorate the Pantheon, Raphael's burial-place, with paintings, this portrait was exhibited, with the universal applause of all the painters, who declared that it alone appeared real, and all the others "paintings"; and on this account he was received as an Academician in 1650. Deciding to return to Spain because of the many letters that the King had sent to his Ambassador ordering his return, he thought of travelling through Paris, and obtained a passport for that purpose from the French Ambassador, but on account of the wars he decided against that course. He embarked at Genoa . . . ; and arrived at Barcelona in June 1651 . . .'* (Palomino).

Documents confirm Palomino's report of the visit. Velasquez was received as an Academician at the famous Academy of Saint Luke in Rome in January 1650. The portrait of *Juan de Pareja* (Plate 36) was apparently exhibited at the Pantheon on the 19th March 1650, and Palomino appears to be mistaken in stating that the portrait preceded his reception as Academician. In February 1650 Velasquez was also enrolled in the *Congregazione dei Virtuosi al Pantheon*. On the 17th February 1650 Philip IV wrote to his Ambassador in Rome: '*. . . for you know Velasquez' phlegm, and it would be well for you to ensure that he departs for Spain as soon as possible after he has completed his mission, at the end of May or the beginning of June . . .*' This was the first of a whole series of letters from the King to his Ambassador urging his painter's return, but another year was to pass before Velasquez started on his return journey. In this letter the King states that part of Velasquez' mission was to arrange for Pietro da Cortona, the most celebrated decorator of the time, to go to Spain; Velasquez was only able to arrange for the frescoists Mitelli and Colonna to go, and it was not until 1658 that they arrived in Madrid. In December 1650 the Cardinal Secretary to the Curia writes to the Papal Nuncio in Spain of Velasquez' desire to receive one of the three Military Orders.

23RD JUNE 1651   The King writes to his Ambassador in Rome advising him of Velasquez' return to the Court.

12TH JULY 1651   Birth of the Infanta Margarita to Philip IV and his new Queen, Mariana. The Infanta is the subject of many of Velasquez' final masterpieces (Plates 40 to 43, and 46).

29TH SEPTEMBER 1651	An order that Velasquez be paid his salary as Painter to the Chamber and as Assistant to the Chamber for the time of his absence in Italy, and that his salary as Superintendent of the King's Works should continue.
16TH FEBRUARY 1652	The six members of the King's special Commission give their recommendations for the vacant post of *Aposentador* of the Palace (Officer of the Court Apartments); three recommend Gaspar de Fuensalida in first place; two, Francisco de Rojas; and one, Alonso Carbonel, the architect who had worked on the Buen Retiro Palace. One member of the Commission gives Velasquez' name as a second choice. The King adds his resolution: 'I nominate Velasquez'; and on the 8th March 1652 he was sworn in to the new post.
1653	Painted the portrait of the *Infanta Margarita*, in a silver and rose dress and with a vase of flowers (Plates 40 and 41).
1655	Painted his last portrait of *Philip IV* (Plate 48).
1655—1656	Painted *Las Meninas* (Plate 43), which includes portraits of the Infanta Margarita, the artist, and reflected in the mirror at the back, Philip IV and his Queen, Mariana. This is his most celebrated work.
1657	Expresses a wish to visit Italy again, but is not granted leave. Mazo, his son-in-law, visits Italy.
6TH JUNE 1658	The King grants Velasquez the Order of Santiago. Before Velasquez could be invested with the Order, many enquiries had to be made involving the testimonies of scores of witnesses in Seville and Madrid and in the border towns nearest to Oporto in Portugal, where his father was born (for Portugal was no longer part of Spain). It was necessary to prove, among other things, that the family on his father's and mother's side was of noble descent, free from admixture of Jewish or Moorish blood, and not contaminated by engaging in trade or commerce. It was only satisfactorily proved that the de Silvas were of noble descent, and Philip IV had to obtain a dispensation from the Pope (Papal Brief of October 1659).
APRIL 1659	Beginning of the decoration of the *Salón de Espejos* (Hall of Mirrors) in the Royal Palace, carried out by Mitelli and Colonna and other artists after plans made by Velasquez. The *Mercury and Argus* (Plate 45) was probably painted as part of the decoration at this time. In 1659 Velasquez makes the portraits of the *Infanta Margarita*, in a blue and silver dress (Plate 46) and of the *Prince Philip Prosper* (Plate 47; the Prince was born on the 28th November 1657, and hopes were placed on him as heir to the Spanish Crown, but he died at the age of four years), which were sent to the Court of Vienna, and '. . . *he took up his brushes only a few times after this; and it can be said that these portraits were his last works, and the last in perfection*' (Palomino).
28TH NOVEMBER 1659	Velasquez invested with the Order of Santiago.
1660	As *Aposentador*, Velasquez makes preparations for the King's journey to the Isle of

32

Pheasants on the Franco-Spanish frontier and for the reception there, on the occasion of the giving in marriage of the Infanta María Teresa to Louis XIV of France. He left Madrid ahead of the King on the 8th April, and returned on the 26th June.

3RD JULY 1660   Velasquez writes to his friend the painter Diego Valentín Díaz in Valladolid: '... *I arrived back at the Court early in the morning on Saturday the 26th June ... I am tired after travelling at night and working during the day, but in good health, and* gracias a Dios, *I found my household in good health too.'*

'*When Velasquez entered his house, he was received by his family and friends with more alarm than joy, for a rumour of his death had reached the Court ... ; and this seemed an omen of the short time he had to live ... On the last day of July, having attended on His Majesty all the morning, he left tired and in pain, and was obliged to return quickly to his apartment ... His Majesty was concerned for his health and ordered his doctors to see him ... On Friday, the 6th August 1660, at two o'clock in the morning, he gave up his Soul ... and was mourned by all, and not least by the King, who had shown during his illness his high estimation and regard for him*' (Palomino).

7TH AUGUST 1660   '*On the 7th August ... Diego Velázquez, Knight of Santiago and Aposentador of His Majesty, died ... and was buried in the vaults of the church*' — Register of Burials, Parish Church of San Juan Bautista, Madrid.

His wife died one week later: '*On the 14th August ... Juana Pacheco, wife of Diego de Silva Velázquez, who lived in the Casa del Tesoro of the Palace, died ...*' — Idem.

FURTHER DATES RELATING TO VELASQUEZ' CAREER

1580	Portugal incorporated under the Spanish Crown. Spain's dominion now stretches over Europe and the whole of the known world.
1588	Defeat of Philip II's 'Invincible' Armada, one of the first shocks to Spain's prestige.
1591	Birth in Valencia of the painter Ribera.
1598	Death of Philip II, and accession of Philip III. Birth in Estremadura of the painter Zurbarán.
1600	Birth of Calderón, to become Philip IV's favourite playwright.
1602	Birth in Granada of the sculptor and painter Alonso Cano.
1603	First visit to the Spanish Court of Rubens; the Court was at the time in Valladolid.
1606	Birth of Rembrandt.
1609	Twelve Years Truce between Spain and the Northern Provinces of the Spanish Netherlands. After a long struggle the Northern Provinces (Holland) are henceforth *de facto* independent of Spain.
1610	*Expulsion of the Moriscos* (converted Moors) from Spain (the subject of Velasquez' lost painting of 1627). This expulsion of hundreds of thousands of industrious citizens had an adverse effect on Spain's economy. Death in Italy of Caravaggio.
1614	Death in Toledo of El Greco.
1616	Death of Cervantes and of Shakespeare.

1617	Birth in Seville of the painter Murillo (baptised 1st January 1618).
1618	Outbreak of the Thirty Years War, involving the Spanish dominions in Europe.
1621	End of the Twelve Years Truce. Spain resumes hostilities against the Northern Provinces. Death of Philip III. Accession of *Philip IV* (born 1605). Plates 10, 12, 13, 19, 20, 21 and 48).
	Olivares becomes the King's Favourite and Chief Minister (Plate 11).
1622	Birth in Seville of the painter Valdés Leal.
1623	Sumptuary regulations at Court substitute the simple collar (*golilla*) for the elaborate ruffs worn in Philip III's reign (see Plate 12).
1625	The town of *Breda* surrendered to Spínola, the Spanish military commander in the Netherlands. This was to be one of the last significant victories gained by Spain. (Plate 21).
1627	Death of the poet *Góngora* (Plate 10).
1629	Spínola is relieved of his command in the Netherlands and is transferred to the Milanese. He dies in Milan in 1630.
	Birth of an heir to the Spanish Crown, the *Prince Baltasar Carlos* (Plates 18 and 22).
1635	Death of the poet and playwright Lope de Vega.
1638	Victory over the French at Fuenterrabía on the Franco-Spanish frontier, postponing by two years the French invasion of Spain.
	Birth of the Dauphin Louis of France, later Louis XIV, and also of the Spanish Princess, the *Infanta María Teresa* (Plate 39), who was later to marry the French King.
1639	Imprisonment of the poet *Quevedo* on the suspicion of attacking Olivares in his verse (Velasquez' portrait is known from replicas).
1640	Death in Flanders of Rubens.
	Revolt of Catalonia (July) and of Portugal (December). The French invade Catalonia and Aragon; and in the following years Philip IV makes annual visits to the Aragonese battle-front. Trans-Pyrenean Catalonia is lost to France. Portugal is *de facto* separated from Spain, and hence also the Portuguese overseas dominions.
1643	Fall of Olivares (January), who dies in retirement 1645.
	Release of Quevedo, who dies 1645.
1644	The town of Lérida in Aragon, occupied by the French, is retaken in the presence of Philip IV (Plate 21). Death of Philip IV's first wife, Isabel.
1646	Death of the Prince Baltasar Carlos, leaving the Spanish Crown without an heir.
1648	Peace of Westphalia, and the end of the Thirty Years War. Holland's independence of Spain recognised. Hostilities between France and Spain continue.
1649	Philip IV marries his niece, *Mariana* (Plate 38).
1651	Birth of a Princess, the *Infanta Margarita*, to Philip IV (Plates 40 to 43, and 46).
1657	Birth of a Prince and heir, *Philip Prosper*, to Philip IV (dies 1661). (Plate 47).
1660	The giving in marriage of the Infanta María Teresa to the French King Louis XIV (9th June), sealing the peace between France and Spain, and confirming Spain's final eclipse as a great power.

34

NOTES ON THE PLATES

All the paintings reproduced are in oil on canvas

Plate 1 Details from *Christ in the House of Martha and Mary*. 23⅝ × 40¾ in. (60 × 103 cm.). *c.* 1617–1618. National Gallery, London.

For the whole painting, see Figure 6. Painted before *The Cook* (Plate 4) which is dated in 1618. One of the earliest of the *bodegones*, it introduces us perhaps more intimately than any other to the young artist's interests soon after he left Pacheco's studio. This particular type of *bodegón*, a painting in which a religious scene is relegated to the background (in this case seen through the hatch), was of Northern origin. Only one other painting of this type by Velasquez is known, the *Servant Girl* in the Beit Collection. Compositionally the painting does not hold together well, and it can be effectively considered as three separate paintings: the religious scene (the presence of Christ in the background of this simple domestic scene is certainly not without meaning and effect; and in both the *bodegones* of this type by Velasquez, the subject chosen is one to which the kitchen scene is appropriate); the portrait; and the still-life. None of the early portrait drawings mentioned by Pacheco has come down to us, but some idea of their nature can be formed from the portrait detail from this painting. There is a remarkable correspondence between this detail and the drawing by Dürer (Figure 2), whose portrait drawings and engravings Pacheco set as

examples to follow. Equally remarkable is Velasquez' approach to the still-life, quite distinct from that of the Northern artists who only provided the criterion for the type of *bodegón* painting, and distinct also from Caravaggio's approach with its formal and decorative suggestions. A source nearer in spirit are the still-lifes painted around 1600 by Sánchez Cotán and admired by Pacheco (Figure 3).

The woman appears again in *The Cook* (Plate 4); and it has been observed that the same model was probably used for the girl in this painting as for the boy in *The Cook*. The still-life objects, such as the pestle and mortar, appear again in *The Cook* and in the *Two men at a table* (Plate 5), and in other *bodegones*.

Plate 2 *The Virgin of the Immaculate Conception*. 53¼ × 40¼ in. (135 × 102 cm.). *c.* 1617–1618. Mrs Phyllis L. Woodall and Miss Frere; on loan to the National Gallery, London.

A pendant to the *Saint John Evangelist on Patmos* (Plate 3). The pair of paintings is first recorded by Ceán in his *Diccionario de las Bellas Artes* (1800), when both were in the Chapter House of the Shod Carmelites in Seville, for which destination they were probably originally painted. This was probably the first official commission received by Velasquez after becoming a master *pintor de imaginería* (the *bodegones*, as far as they were commissioned, were made for private patrons). The handling of the rather heavy, 'leathery' paint would derive in part from Velasquez' experience in the painting of sculpture. The pose of the Virgin and the symbols introduced were proper to the interpretation of the Mystery, and are as described in Pacheco's *Arte de la Pintura* (including the moon 'with the points downwards', recommended by Pacheco in place of the more conventional method of showing them pointing upwards). In 1630 Pacheco made a painting of the subject identical in composition, and it would seem that both master and pupil knew some common prototype in sculpture or engraving. The Virgin was certainly painted from a model, although the portrait quality is appropriately less evident than in the *bodegones*, and it is likely that the model was Velasquez' young wife or wife-to-be (married in 1618). She appears again, a year or two older, in the *Adoration of the Kings* of 1619 (Plate 6). The subject was the most popular one at this time in Spain.

Plate 3 *Saint John Evangelist on Patmos.* $53\frac{1}{4} \times 40\frac{1}{4}$ in. $(135 \times 102$ cm.$)$. *c.* 1617–1618. National Gallery, London.
A pendant to the *Virgin of the Immaculate Conception* (Plate 2), which Mystery was related to Saint John's vision of the Miraculous Woman. The technique of the two paintings is identical. The comparatively hard modelling and the treatment of the drapery folds in both paintings recall Pacheco (Figure 5 is from a series of Evangelists; it is dated in 1632, but Pacheco's style changed little from the early years of the century). It has been suggested that the model for the Saint was the young artist himself.

Plate 4 *The Cook.* 39×46 in. $(99 \times 117$ cm.$)$. Dated 1618. National Gallery of Scotland, Edinburgh.
The earliest dated painting, and the earliest precisely datable. The boy appears in a number of Velasquez' paintings at this time (see Plates 6 and 7, and possibly Plate 1), and is probably to be identified with the 'young country lad' who, Pacheco tells us, Velasquez hired as a model. The old woman appears again in the *Christ in the House of Martha and Mary* (Plate 1).

The painting was one of the four *bodegones* described by Palomino (1724). The easier unity of the painting suggest thats it was executed somewhat later than the *Christ in the House of Martha and Mary* (Plate 1 and Figure 6). The rather high view-point was commonly employed by the sixteenth-century Northern masters, such as Aertsen, Beuckelaer and Hemessen, who provided the prototype for this *genre* of painting.

Plate 5 *Two men at a table.* 25×40 in. $(63 \times 102$ cm.$)$. *c.* 1619–1620. Wellington Museum, London.
One of the four *bodegones* described by Palomino (1724). With *The Waterseller* (Plate 7) it was presented to the Duke of Wellington by King Ferdinand VII of Spain. In this *bodegón*, one of the last he painted, the simple and effective composition, depending on the correspondence of the group of two figures and the still-life group, conveys something of the quiet and intimate atmosphere of the scene.

Plate 6 Detail from the *Adoration of the Kings.* $78\frac{7}{8} \times 49\frac{1}{2}$ in. $(203 \times 125$ cm.$)$. Dated 1619. Museo del Prado, Madrid.
For the whole painting, see Figure 1. Painted for the Jesuit Church of the Noviciado de San Luis, Seville. The painting is the one most reminiscent of Caravaggio in composition and lighting. The simple and effective compositional *motif* of the Virgin and Child is Velasquez' own, and the inspiration for it may have been derived from Montañés' contemporary carvings in relief. The models for the Virgin and the Child were almost certainly Velasquez' young wife and their first child, born in 1619. The boy on the left (see Figure 1) appears in a number of Velasquez' *bodegones* (see Plates 4 and 7, and possibly Plate 1).

Plate 7 *The Waterseller.* $41\frac{1}{2} \times 31\frac{1}{2}$ in. $(105 \times 80.)$ cm. *c.* 1619–1620. Wellington Museum, London.
The most celebrated, and certainly the most impressive, of the *bodegones*. One of the four described by Palomino (1724). This painting was among those captured by the British from the train of Joseph Bonaparte fleeing after his defeat at Vitoria (1813), and presented to the Duke of Wellington by King Ferdinand VII of Spain. The boy on the left appears in

a number of the *bodegones* (see Plate 4), and he and the waterseller appear in the *Adoration of the Kings* (see Figure 1).

Plate 8 *Saint Thomas Apostle.* $38\frac{1}{2} \times 30\frac{3}{4}$ in. $(98 \times 78$ cm.$)$. *c.* 1620. Musée des Beaux-Arts, Orleans. The painting is inscribed top left: *S. TOMAS*. Apparently from a series of Apostles, and possibly to be identified with the series seen by Ponz (1776) in the Carthusian Monastery of Nuestra Señora de las Cuevas, Seville, attributed locally to Velasquez. The model for the Saint is possibly the same as for the *Saint John Evangelist* (Plate 3), considered by some to be the artist himself. A *Saint Paul Apostle* from the same series is in the Barcelona Museum. The *Apostolado* (a series of the twelve Apostles and Christ, as full-length figures or otherwise) was possibly the most common subject commissioned from an artist in Spain after the representations of the Virgin and Christ.

Plate 9 Detail from the full-length portrait of *Jerónima de la Fuente.* $63 \times 43\frac{1}{2}$ in. $(160 \times 110$ cm.$)$. Signed and dated 1620. Museo del Prado, Madrid.
This and a posthumous portrait of *Cristóbal Suárez de Ribera* (church of San Hermenegildo, Seville), also signed and dated in 1620, are the earliest independent portraits known by Velasquez. The Franciscan nun was in Seville from the 1st to 20th June 1620 on her way to Mexico and the Philippines, where she founded the Convent of Santa Clara in Manila, and the portrait is accordingly precisely datable. Velasquez painted another version of the portrait, in which the Crucifix is turned partly towards the spectator (in the collection of Alejandro Fernando de Araoz, Madrid). Velasquez was to retain the simplicity of pose in his portraits throughout his career.

Plate 10 *Luis de Góngora.* 20×16 in. $(51 \times 41$ cm.$)$. 1622. Museum of Fine Arts, Boston, Mass.
The great Spanish poet (1561–1627) was born in Córdova; moved to the Court in 1612, and was appointed Chaplain to the King; and died in Madrid. The portrait was painted for Pacheco on Velasquez' preliminary visit to Madrid in the spring of 1622.

It is interesting to compare this portrait, with its broader and more simplified modelling in planes, with the *Jerónima de la Fuente* (Plate 9), painted two years previously in Seville, with its comparatively detailed and literal description of the features.

Plate 11 Detail from the full-length portrait of *Olivares.* $87\frac{1}{2} \times 54$ in. $(222 \times 137$ cm.$)$. Dated 1625. Hispanic Society of America, New York.
The Count-Duke of Olivares (1587–1645), Philip IV's Favourite and Chief Minister until his disgrace in January 1643. The treatment of the portrait is a grand development of that of the *Góngora* (Plate 10), painted three years previously, and the comparative schematic effect of the earlier portrait, with its harder modelling and the somewhat abrupt transitions between the planes, has disappeared.

Plate 12 *Philip IV.* $79\frac{1}{2} \times 40\frac{1}{2}$ in. $(202 \times 103$ cm.$)$. 1624. Metropolitan Museum, New York (Bequest of Benjamin Altman).
Painted by December 1624, when Velasquez was paid for three portraits ordered by Antonia de Ipeñarrieta: of her husband (lost), the *King* (this portrait) and *Olivares* (São Paolo). It certainly records Velasquez' first portrait of the King completed on the 30th August 1623, shortly after his arrival at the Court, for the King would not have sat again for a private commission and it is only reasonable to believe that Velasquez copied his earlier portrait for Antonia de Ipeñarrieta. The King is portrayed at the age of eighteen or nineteen (he was born in 1605). Velasquez had studied the great masterpieces of portraiture in the royal collections, including works by Titian and the great Venetians, and probably sought to emulate them, but there is little that recalls any acquaintanceship with the colour and free handling of Venetian painting. The simple and rather austere elegance accorded with the atmosphere of the Court at the time: black was prescribed for the dress at Court, and on Velasquez' arrival at Court, soon after Philip IV's accession, sumptuary regulations substituted the simple collar (the *golilla*, worn by the King in this portrait) for the elaborate ruffs worn in the previous reign. The employment of the light background,

giving an impression of space and air surrounding the figure, is an innovation.

Plate 13 *Philip IV*. 79 × 40 in. (201 × 102 cm.). *c.* 1626. Museo del Prado, Madrid.

The lines of the 1623 portrait (see note to Plate 12) have long been visible beneath this portrait of the King, and it has been recognised that Velasquez started with his first design. X-rays now point to the possibility of this portrait having been painted over his 'lost' first portrait of the King. In the three years that separate the two portraits, a considerable advance has been made in the modelling of the features, in the treatment of light and in the suggestion of atmosphere. The present poor condition of the painting obscures the original simple and impressive design. Three details have been chosen to illustrate the advance made during his first few years at court.

Plate 14 Detail from *The Drinkers* (*Los Borrachos*). 65 × 88½ in. (165 × 225 cm.). *c.* 1626 – 1628. Museo del Prado, Madrid.

The Triumph of Bacchus was popularly called *The Drinkers*. Ponz (1776) describes it as a '*Trionfo de Baco en ridículo*', that is, a burlesque interpretation of the theme. This was Velasquez' first mythological painting. He received payment for it from the King in July 1629, but it was probably painted a year or two earlier. The scene of Bacchus presiding over the revellers is intended to take place in the open, but at this stage in Velasquez' development there is little suggestion of depth, and the sky acts more or less as a back-cloth. His lost equestrian portrait of Philip IV of 1625 is recorded to have been painted against a landscape background, and likewise his lost first history painting, the *Expulsion of the Moriscos*, of 1627, and the assumption must be that he was no more successful in these. From the year 1630, when he was first in Italy, to 1635, when he painted the *Surrender of Breda* (see Plates 15 to 17 and 20 to 23), he made the greatest advances in solving problems of space. Velasquez was never happy with the mythological narrative unless he could interpret it in terms of everyday and present reality, and in this composition — the earliest of his with many figures, and

the first of his mythological paintings — in which the Caravaggesque figure of the god is derived from a sixteenth-century print, and the figures on the left apparently from some Venetian painting, the one really successful part of the painting is the sympathetically observed group of drinkers and the figure of the man seeking alms, reproduced in this detail.

Plate 15 *The Forge of Vulcan*. 88 × 114 in. (223 × 290 cm.). 1630. Museo del Prado, Madrid.

Painted in Rome in 1630, and bought by Philip IV in 1634. Apollo visits Vulcan with the news of Vulcan's wife Venus' adultery with Mars. This painting illustrates the advance made in the depiction of space and atmosphere in the three or four years following the *Bacchus* (Plate 14). Velasquez has succeeded in relating the subject to an everyday scene in a forge. The flow of reaction to Apollo's announcement, passing through Vulcan and his companions, is superbly expressed.

Plate 16 *View of the Garden of the Villa Medici, Rome*. 19 × 16½ in. (48 × 42 cm.). 1630 or 1649 – 1651. Museo del Prado, Madrid.

Painted on the same occasion as the *View* reproduced in the following plate, and probably in 1630 on his first visit to Italy when he was staying at the Villa Medici and was concerned with problems of space and atmosphere, rather than on his second visit, when he was in Rome from 1649 to 1651. These two *Views* are the only independent landscapes certainly known by Velasquez. In the few years after his return from his first visit to Italy he set many of his portraits in spacious landscapes (the 'hunting' portraits and equestrian portraits of *c.* 1632 – 1635; Plates 20 and 23). To R. A. M. Stevenson (*Art of Velasquez*, 1895) these *Views* recalled Corot. The shadows and the quality of the light indicate that this view was painted in the evening.

Plate 17 *View of the Garden of the Villa Medici, Rome*. 17¼ × 15 in. (44 × 38 cm.). 1630 or 1649 – 1651. Museo del Prado, Madrid.

Painted on the same occasion as the *View* reproduced on Plate 16. It was apparently painted at midday.

Plate 18 *Prince Baltasar Carlos and his Dwarf.* 53½ × 41 in. (136 × 104 cm.). 1631. Museum of Fine Arts, Boston, Mass.

The Prince, born on 17th October 1629 during Velasquez' absence from the Court on his visit to Italy, appears to be about one and a half to two years of age, and the portrait was accordingly painted shortly after Velasquez' return from Italy in 1631, as recorded by Pacheco. The dwarf, '*El Niño de Vallecas*', was painted again by Velasquez around 1644 (Plate 33).

Plate 19 *Philip IV (The 'Silver' Philip).* 77 × 43 in. (195 × 110 cm.). Signed. *c.* 1632−1636. National Gallery, London.

The King is dressed in brown and silver. He is portrayed at the age of about twenty-eight years. The painting is signed on the paper held in the King's hand: ' . . . *Diego Velasquez* . . .', and is one of the very few paintings that he signed. In 1888, Justi read the date 1636, but there is no trace now, and there does not seem to be any space for a date. The same portrait and essentially the same pose were employed in the portrait of *Philip IV in hunting dress* (Prado), of similar date. A comparison with the earlier portraits of the King (Plates 12 and 13) will illustrate the advance made in the freedom of handling, and in the extension of his palette.

Plate 20 *Philip IV on horseback.* 118 × 124 in. (301 × 314 cm.). 1634−1635. Museo del Prado, Madrid.

The King on a rearing horse is portrayed against the distant background of the Guadarrama mountains, north of Madrid. Painted to take its place in the decoration of the *Gran Salón* of the newly built Buen Retiro Palace in Madrid, in which all the leading artists at the Court were involved, and to which Velasquez contributed the five equestrian portraits of the reigning King (this painting), the Queen and the Prince (Plate 22) and Philip III and his Queen, and the *Surrender of Breda* (Plate 21). The portraits of Philip IV and his wife flanked the entrance door to the *Salón*, the Prince's portrait was above the door and those of Philip III and his wife hung on either side of the throne opposite. The twelve battle-pieces,

including Velasquez' *Surrender of Breda*, were hung on the two long walls between the windows. These works for the Buen Retiro represent the culmination of the central phase of his development, in which he was especially concerned with problems of space and of the expression of external movement and grandeur of effect. This corresponded in time with a similar culmination in Baroque painting generally. Velasquez characteristically does not fill his sky with allegorical figures, or introduce great floating draperies − but the sense of grandeur and energy, and certainly the sense of reality, is not thereby impaired. Velasquez was not to repeat the splendid spacious backgrounds of his equestrian paintings. The equestrian portrait of the King provided the model for the bronze equestrian statue made by the Florentine sculptor Pietro Tacca which was placed at the entrance to the great courtyard of the Buen Retiro Palace (little remains now of the Palace and the statue has been moved to front the Royal Palace); and incidentally helped finally to solve the problem which earlier had interested Leonardo da Vinci, of designing a monumental, free-standing statue with rearing horse. Tacca's original design did not satisfy the King and his Minister, and it was decided to have the horse modelled on Velasquez' painting, for which purpose Velasquez sent Tacca a copy of his painting, and the Sevillian sculptor Montañés was brought from Seville to model the bust of the King (see Plate 24). Galileo was also involved in the solution of this problem (in addition to the King, Velasquez and the great sculptors of Spain and Italy, Montañés and Tacca), being consulted on the problem of stability.

Plate 21 *The Surrender of Breda* (Las Lanzas). 121 × 145 in. (307 × 367 cm.). 1634 − 1635. Museo del Prado, Madrid.

Popularly called *Las Lanzas*, with references to the wall of lances on the right of the painting. One of the most celebrated paintings in European art, and the masterpiece of Velasquez' middle period. The *Surrender of Breda* was one of the twelve paintings of the military successes of Philip IV's reign contributed by the leading painters at the Court to the decoration of the new Palace of the Buen Retiro (see note to Plate 20). Breda surrendered to the Spanish in June 1625 Characteristically, Velasquez interprets the scene in purely human terms and choses the incident after the fall of the citadel, when Justin of Nassau hands the keys of the town to Spínola, the Spanish commander. Velasquez accompanied Spínola to Italy in 1629, and probably made a sketch of him on that occasion. The reactions of the victors and vanquished are centred around the magnanimous gesture of the great Spanish general and nobleman who has fulfiled, the King's order, 'Marquis, you will take Breda'! and who pays homage to the courage of the vanquished. X-ray photographs show that considerable adjustments were made in the course of executing the painting; and, in particular, the horse on the right (an important compositional *motif*, leading the eye into the painting) was an afterthought.

Plate 22 Detail from the portrait of *Prince Baltasar Carlos on horseback*. 82½ × 68 in. (209 × 173 cm.). 1634—1635. Museo del Prado, Madrid.
Painted for the *Gran Salón* of the Buen Retiro Palace, and completed, with the other works for the same destination, by June 1635 (see note to Plate 20). Probably the last of the equestrian portraits to be completed. The detail illustrates the freedom of his technique at this central stage of his career.

Plate 23 *Prince Baltasar Carlos in hunting dress.* 75 × 40½ in. (191 × 103 cm.). 1635—1636. Museo del Prado, Madrid.
An inscription gives the age of the Prince (born on 17th October 1629) as six years. With the portraits of *Philip IV* and the *Cardinal Infante Ferdinand* in hunting dress (both Prado), probably painted some time before, destined for the Torre de la Parada, the royal hunting lodge near Madrid. In this painting and the equestrian portraits he finally solves the problem of space, and they are the last in which he employs a spacious setting.

Plate 24 *Juan Martínez Montañés.* 46 × 34¼ in. (109 × 87 cm.). 1635—1636. Museo del Prado, Madrid.

The great sculptor (1568—1649) from Seville, with whom Velasquez was acquainted in his youth, was in Madrid from June 1635 to early 1636 to model the head of the King for Pietro Tacca's bronze equestrian statue (see note to Plate 20). In the portrait he is shown working on the model. The painting is not to be considered unfinished — the sketched-in model of the King's head is intentionally not allowed to compete with that of the artist. Particularly impressive is the *motif* of the sculptor's hand poised with the modelling tools as he momentarily glances away from his work.

Plate 25 *The Crucified Christ.* 97½ × 70 in. (248 × 169 cm.). *c.* 1636. Museo del Prado, Madrid. Painted for the Church of San Plácido, Madrid. One of the most moving interpretations of the subject, and certainly Velasquez' masterpiece in religious painting. It is close to Montañés' *Crucified Christ* carved 1603—1606 (see Figure 4). Velasquez knew well Montañés' masterpiece in Seville Cathedral, and probably knew the terms of the contract, for such things would have been discussed at the gatherings in his master's house. That Baroque quality of presence demanded in the contract for the carving (quoted on page 10) is hardly present in Montañés' work and is first achieved in Velasquez' painting.

Plate 26 *The Coronation of the Virgin.* 69 × 49 in. (176 × 124 cm.). *c.* 1640. Museo del Prado, Madrid. Painted for the Oratory of Queen Isabel in the Royal Palace. There is a splendour of colour and handling in this essentially devotional and decorative work. A number of possible sources have been suggested for the composition, which is certainly not original.

Plate 27 *Portrait of a lady with a fan* (The artist's daughter, Francisca?). 36¼ × 26¾ in. (92 × 68 cm.). *c.* 1640—1648. Wallace Collection, London.
If it represents the artist's daughter, who was born in 1619, the portrait could not have been painted much before 1648. The artist's wife has also been considered, who was thirty-eight years of age in 1640, and the portrait could hardly have been painted much before that date. The portrait employs the same pose

as that in the Chatsworth Collection, which shows the same sitter a few years younger.

Plate 28 *Aesop.* 71 × 37 in. (179 × 94 cm.). *c.* 1640. Museo del Prado, Madrid.

The painting is inscribed top left: *AESOPVS.* A pendant to the *Menippus* (Prado), and destined to decorate the Torre de la Parada, the royal hunting lodge near Madrid. Both of these paintings of 'beggar philosophers' are remarkable character studies, and in each case it seems that Velasquez has carefully chosen and portrayed a model whom he knew to possess the appropriate character.

Plate 29 *The Court Fool 'Calabacillas'.* 42 × 32¾ in. (106 × 83 cm.). *c.* 1639—1644. Museo del Prado, Madrid.

A detail from one of the four portraits of Court Fools painted around 1644 (see Plates 30, 32 and 33) which constitute Velasquez' greatest achievement in the years preceding his second visit to Italy. The dwarf is shown full-length and seated, like the others in the series. Velasquez made a portrait of the same Fool in the 1620's (Cook Collection, Edinburgh). The sitter died in October 1639, and this portrait must have been started about that time. These Court Fools are not made the subject of caricature or ridicule, nor does Velasquez enlist our pity for their occupation or their deformities; instead each is a penetrating and sympathetic portrait of an individual, and fundamentally his approach is the same when he paints the portrait of the King (Plate 31; this portrait of Philip IV was painted at the same time as the series of dwarfs).

Plate 30 *The Court Fool 'El Primo'.* 42 × 32¼ in. (107 × 82 cm.). 1644. Museo del Prado, Madrid.

One of the four portraits of Court Fools painted around 1644 (see Plate 29 and Note, and Plates 32 and 33). The only one of the series precisely datable, it was painted in June 1644 in Fraga, on the same occasion as the 'Fraga' Philip (Plate 31). The books refer to his employment also in clerical work at the Court.

Plate 31 *Philip IV (The 'Fraga' Philip).* 53¼ × 38½ in. (135 × 98 cm.). 1644. Frick Collection, New York.

The King is portrayed at the age of 39 years. Painted in Fraga in June 1644, when Velasquez accompanied the King on his campaign to Aragon. The King appears in the red and silver uniform he wore on the campaign. The quiet splendour of the colour and light, and the brilliance of the handling foreshadow the *Innocent X* (Plate 37) of 1650 and the series of portraits of the young *Princess Margarita* (Plates 40 to 42, and 46) painted in the last years of his life.

Plate 32 *The Court Fool Sebastián de Morra.* 41¾ × 32 in. (106 × 81 cm.). *c.* 1644. Museo del Prado, Madrid.

One of the four portraits of Court Fools painted around 1644 (see Plate 29 and Note, and Plates 30 and 33). Sebastián de Morra came to the Court from Flanders in 1643.

Plate 33 Detail from the portrait of the Court Fool *'El Niño de Vallecas'.* 42 × 32½ in. (107 × 83 cm.). *c.* 1644. Museo del Prado, Madrid.

A detail from one of the four portraits of Court Fools painted around 1644 (see Plate 29 and Note, and Plates 30 and 32). The dwarf is shown full-length and seated like the others in the series. The same dwarf accompanies Prince Baltasar Carlos in Velasquez' painting of 1631 (Plate 18).

Plate 34 *Mars.* 71 × 37½ in. (179 × 95 cm.). *c.* 1640—1644. Museo del Prado, Madrid.

This burlesque interpretation of the pagan god was painted for the Torre de la Parada, the royal hunting lodge near Madrid. The general idea of the nude figure of the god, wearing his helmet and with armour at his feet, was possibly taken from an Antique marble group that Velasquez knew when he stayed at the Villa Medici in Rome in 1630 and of which he brought back a cast on his return from his final visit to Rome. Here the resemblance ends. The tired and brooding god of War is far from the heroic, classical conception of the god; *Mars* was painted at the time when, following their numerous reverses at the hands of the

French, the remnants of Spain's once proud legions wandered over the countryside of Europe and the homeland (as we see them depicted in Callot's *Les misères de la guerre*).

Plate 35 *Venus*. $48\frac{1}{4} \times 69\frac{3}{4}$ in. (123×177 cm.). *c.* 1640−1648. National Gallery, London.

One of his most celebrated paintings. As it was included in an inventory in Madrid, dated before Velasquez' return from Italy in 1651, it must have been painted before he left for Italy at the end of 1648. It was certainly painted from a model, and in the inventory mentioned is simply called 'a nude woman'. It has been observed, however, that the general idea for the pose was borrowed from a sixteenth-century engraving. Characteristically, adjustments were made in the course of executing the work, and it has been noticed that originally the painting was closer to the engraving than now. It is one of the very few paintings of the nude in Spanish art. Around 1800, Goya, inspired in part by this painting, which was then in the possession of the Duchess of Alba, painted his nude and clothed *Maja*. The three paintings were together as part of Godoy's sequestrated estate in January 1808; and Goya's two paintings, and possibly Velasquez' *Venus*, were among the 'four obscene paintings belonging to Godoy' referred to by the Inquisitor General of the Court in November 1814. In 1914, the painting was slashed in the National Gallery by a suffragette demonstrator.

Plate 36 *Juan de Pareja*. 30×25 in. (76×63 cm.). 1650. The Rt. Hon. the Earl of Radnor, Longford Castle.

Velasquez' assistant, who accompanied him on his second visit to Italy, became a painter in his own right after his master's death. Painted shortly before the *Innocent X* (Plate 37), it was exhibited in the Pantheon, Rome, on the 19th March 1650, and received the applause of 'all the artists in Rome'. The choice of a particular light and of a particular harmony of colours — and hence of a particular manner of painting — appropriate to the subject was fundamental to Velasquez' method of painting. There is a vast difference between the effect achieved in this portrait of Velasquez' assistant and in the portrait of the Pope, *Innocent X*, painted on the same occasion: the present painting with its heavy earth colours based on the green, its subdued light, and the slow and energetic rhythm of the brushwork; the other with its brilliant harmony of reds, gold and white, and the splendour and activity of the light and handling.

Plate 37 *Pope Innocent X*. $55 \times 47\frac{1}{2}$ in. (140×120 cm.). Signed. 1650. Galleria Doria Pamphili, Rome.

Velasquez' most famous portrait, and one of the supreme masterpieces both of portraiture and painting. It is signed on the paper held in the Pope's hand: *... Diego de Silva Velasquez ...*, and is one of only three or four paintings that he signed (another is the so-called '*Silver*' *Philip*, Plate 20). It was painted shortly after the *Juan de Pareja* (Plate 36). The not too prepossessing Pope recognised Velasquez' great achievement in this portrait, which was followed by commissions to Velasquez to paint the portraits of the papal household (almost all lost). He presented Velasquez with a gold medallion and chain, intervened through the Papal Nuncio in Madrid to let Velasquez' desire to be invested with one of the three military knighthoods of Spain be known there — and is recorded to have made the discerning compliment that the portrait was '*troppo vero*' ('too faithful').

Plate 38 *Queen Mariana*. $91 \times 51\frac{1}{2}$ in. (231×131 cm.). 1652−1653. Museo del Prado, Madrid.

Philip IV's second wife, daughter of the Emperor Ferdinand III of Austria and Philip IV's sister María. She was born 1634, married her uncle in October 1649 (during Velasquez' absence in Italy) and died in 1696. A replica of the portrait was sent to the Court of Vienna in February 1653. This portrait of Philip IV's new young Queen initiates a whole series of masterpieces (Plates 40 to 43, and 46 and 47).

Plate 39 Detail from the nearly full-length portrait of the *Infanta María Teresa*. $50 \times 38\frac{1}{2}$ in. (127×98 cm). 1653. Kunsthistorisches Museum, Vienna.

The daughter of Philip IV and his first wife, Isabel. She was born 1638, married Louis XIV of France on

9th June 1660 and died in 1683. The portrait was sent to the Court of Vienna in February 1653. This and the following two details illustrate the brilliance of his technique, and the captivating quality of colour and light of his last works. The new harmonies of colour — silvers, blues and rose — are appropriate to the portrayal of the young Princesses at the Court.

Plates 40 and 41 Details from the full-length portrait of the *Infanta Margarita*. 50 × 39½ in. (128 × 100 cm.). 1653. Kunsthistorisches Museum, Vienna.

The daughter of Philip IV and his second wife, Mariana. She was born 12th July 1651, shortly after Velasquez' return from Italy, and appears in this portrait to be about two years of age. See also Plates 42, 43 and 46.

Plate 42 *The Infanta Margarita*. 41½ × 34½ in. (105 × 87 cm.). 1655 – 1656. Kunsthistorisches Museum, Vienna.

For the Infanta, see also Plates 40, 41 and 46. She appears to be about the same age as in *Las Meninas* (Plate 43), or possibly slightly younger, and she wears a similar dress.

Plate 43 *The Maids of Honour (Las Meninas)*. 125 × 109 in. (318 × 276 cm.). 1656. Museo del Prado, Madrid.

The most celebrated of his paintings, and one of the great individual masterpieces of all time. Originally called *La Familia*. The King and Queen are reflected in the mirror in the background. In the centre foreground is their daughter, the Infanta Margarita (see Plate 42, and Plates 40, 41 and 46), with her two Maids of Honour (*Meninas*), the one on her right offering her a cup of water. In the right foreground are her two dwarfs, Marbárbola and the boy Nicolasito, and the dog. Behing this group stand a Lady-in-Waiting, in nun's habit, and a *guardadamas*. In the open doorway in the background is the *Aposentador* of the Queen (Velasquez had been appointed *Aposentador* of the King in 1652). The painter stands at a large canvas. Palomimo (1724) considered that the mirror reflected the King and Queen on Velasquez'

canvas; in any case, it seems to be intended that they are present. The apparent dimensions of the canvas make it possible that Velasquez was painting this double portrait or the picture of 'The Family' itself. The Cross of the Order of Santiago on Velasquez' breast was added later (he received the Order three years after the painting was finished).

Plate 44 Detail from *The Spinners ('Las Hilanderas')*. 85 × 114 in. (220 × 289 cm.). *c.* 1657? Museo del Prado, Madrid.

For the whole painting, see Figure 7. A document recently discovered gives the original title of the painting as *The Story of Arachne*. Arachne competes with Pallas in the weaving of a series of tapestries, of which the *Rape of Europa*, which appears in the background, was the first to be made (Velasquez has followed Titian's painting of the *Rape of Europa*, which was in the Royal collection at the time). Arachne is transformed into a spider. The atmosphere of quiet industry, in the foreground, and of the transformation scene that takes place in the background (not actually shown), is effectively expressed by his employment of light. The spinning-wheel in motion is a remarkable introduction, and helps both to give a quality of reality to the light, and to convey the sound of the quiet activity in the workshop. It has been pointed out convincingly that the general idea for the arrangement of the two seated figures in the foreground, flanking the rectangle of the alcove, was taken from the two *ignudi* on the ceiling of the Sistine Chapel in Rome, which similarly flank a rectangular scene of *God dividing the earth from the waters*. The correspondence is made very clear if one discounts the later addition to the canvas of the strip above the easily visible seam (see Figure 7).

Pacheco says that Velasquez made copies from the paintings in the Sistine Chapel, and the present painting probably used one of these studies made after Michelangelo's ceiling. A date before Velasquez' second visit to Italy has recently been suggested for the painting, in place of the hitherto generally accepted date of *c.* 1657.

Plate 45 Detail from the *Mercury and Argus*.

$50 \times 97\frac{1}{2}$ in. (127×248 cm.). 1659. Museo del Prado, Madrid.

The detail is of the sleeping figure of Argus. Apparently painted as part of the decoration of the *Salón de Espejos* (Hall of Mirrors) in the Royal Palace, which was carried out in 1659.

Plate 46 *The Infanta Margarita.* 50×42 in. (127×107 cm.). 1659. Kunsthistorisches Museum, Vienna.

For the Infanta, see also Plates 40, 41, 42 and 43. Painted as a pendant to the *Philip Prosper* (Plate 47), and both portraits sent to the Court of Vienna in 1659.

Plate 47 *Prince Philip Prosper.* 50×39 in. (128×99 cm.). 1659. Kunsthistorisches Museum, Vienna.
The son of Philip IV and his second wife, Mariana.

He was born November 1658, and died in November 1661. Painted as a pendant to the *Infanta Margarita* (Plate 46), and both portraits sent to the Court of Vienna in 1659. The two portraits were the last to be finished by Velasquez, 'and the last in perfection' (Palomino).

Plate 48 *Philip IV.* 27×22 in. (69×56 cm.). 1655. Museo del Prado, Madrid.

Probably painted 1655 when an engraving was made after it. The last portrait known of the King entirely by Velasquez' hand, with the exception of the portrait in *Las Meninas*.

The version in the National Gallery, London, in which the King appears to be a little older, was probably completed in the dress by an assistant. For other portraits of the King, see Plates 12, 13, 19, 20 and 31.

2

4

5

TOMAS·

8

12

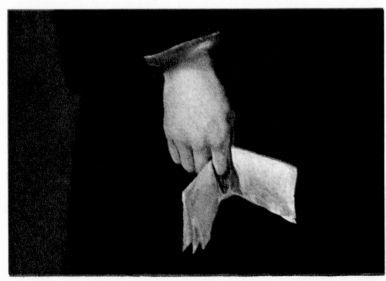

14

15

16

19

20

21

22

23

24

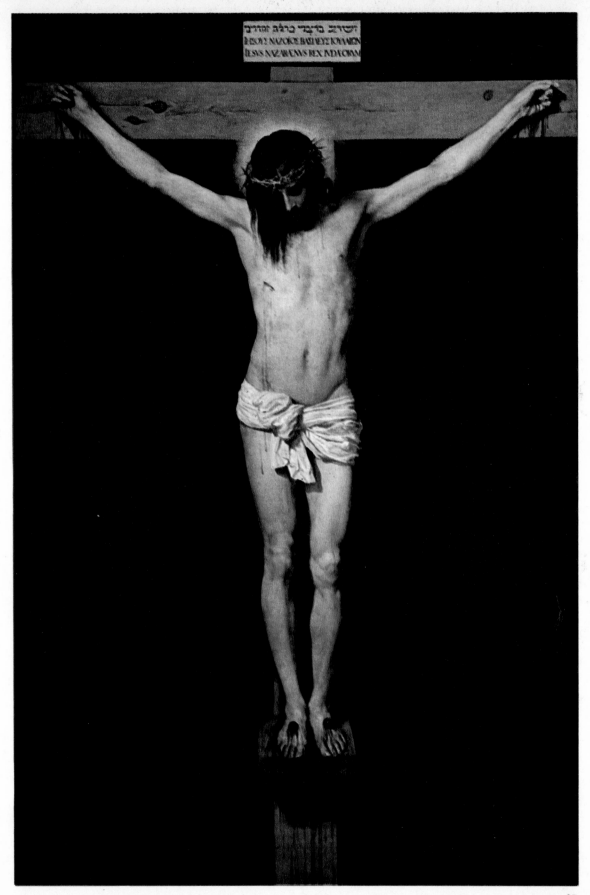

26

32

34

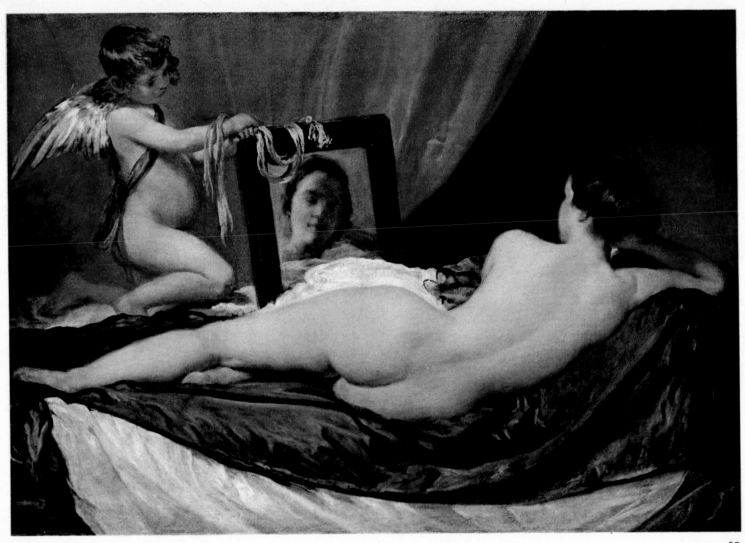

36

38

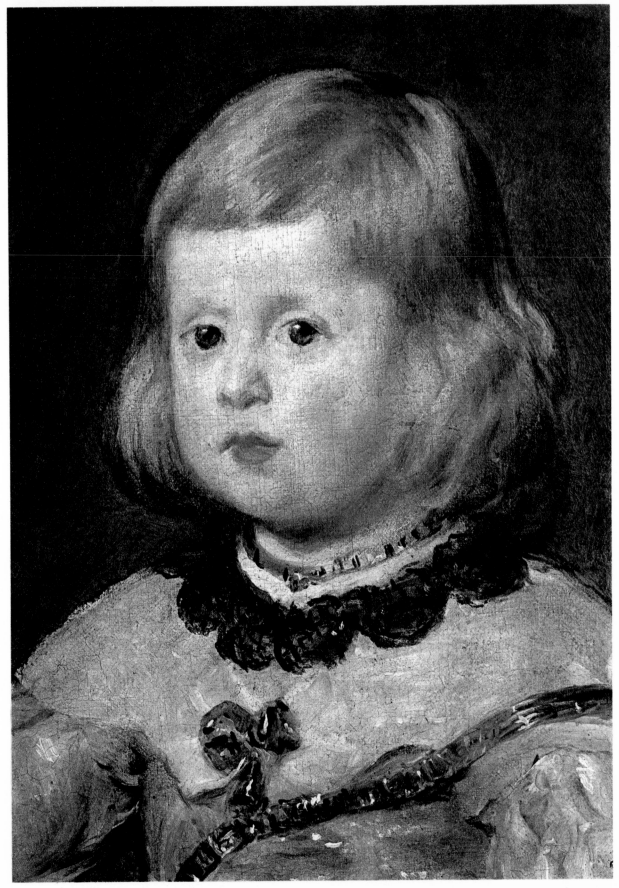

44

45